DOVER · THRIFT · EDITIONS

Faust

Part One

JOHANN WOLFGANG
VON GOETHE

Translated by Anna Swanwick

DOVER PUBLICATIONS, INC.
New York

DOVER THRIFT EDITIONS

GENERAL EDITOR: STANLEY APPELBAUM
EDITOR OF THIS VOLUME: CANDACE WARD

Copyright

Published in Canada by General Publishing Company, Ltd., 30 Lesmill Road, Don Mills, Toronto, Ontario.
Published in the United Kingdom by Constable and Company, Ltd., 3 The Lanchesters, 162–164 Fulham Palace Road, London W6 9ER.

Bibliographical Note

This Dover edition, first published in 1994, contains the unabridged text of *Faust, Part I*, as translated by Anna Swanwick, as published in Volume 19 of *The Harvard Classics*, in 1909 by P.F. Collier & Son Company, New York. Footnotes and an introductory note have been specially prepared for this edition.

Library of Congress Cataloging-in-Publication Data

Goethe, Johann Wolfgang von, 1749–1832.
    [Faust. 1. Theil. English]
    Faust. Part one / Johann Wolfgang von Goethe ; translated by Anna Swanwick.
    p.   cm. — (Dover thrift editions)
    ISBN 0-486-28046-2
    I. Swanwick, Anna, 1813–1899.   II. Title.   III. Series.
PT2026.F2S91   1994
832'.6—dc20   94-20369
                                                                       CIP

Manufactured in the United States of America
Dover Publications, Inc., 31 East 2nd Street, Mineola, N.Y. 11501

Note

JOHANN WOLFGANG VON GOETHE — critic, journalist, painter, theater manager, statesman, novelist, poet, playwright, scientist and philosopher — was born on August 28, 1749, in Frankfurt am Main. Though his formal education ostensibly prepared him for a career in law, and though he held a variety of political posts, Goethe is most famous for the genius of his literary output. Two of his most powerful early works, written during the *Sturm und Drang* movement, were his drama *Götz von Berlichingen* (1773) and the novel *Die Leiden des jungen Werthers (The Sorrows of Young Werther;* 1774).

Perhaps his most well known work, the two-part dramatic poem *Faust,* is an example of Goethe's ability to integrate a wide array of literary and philosophical influences within a dramatic framework. Drawing from a variety of poetic elements — epic, lyric, dramatic, operatic and balletic — the poem also contains a broad range of theatrical styles, including classical Greek tragedy, medieval mystery, Renaissance masque and commedia dell'arte. The story of Faust, one of the most enduring in Western literature, features the German necromancer who sells his soul to the devil in exchange for knowledge and power. In Goethe's version, Faust is both humane and rational; Part One (1808) presents Faust's despair, his pact with Mephistopheles and his tragic relationship with Gretchen. The latter becomes the basis for his eventual redemption in Part Two (published posthumously in 1832), which was a departure from the traditional tragedy of Faust's damnation. Goethe's poem is much more than a retelling of an ancient legend, however; it is the author's commentary on the whole of Western civilization.

Contents

v

DEDICATION

Ye wavering shapes, again ye do enfold me,
As erst upon my troubled sight ye stole;
Shall I this time attempt to clasp, to hold ye?
Still for the fond illusion yearns my soul?
Ye press around! Come then, your captive hold me,
As upward from the vapoury mist ye roll;
Within my breast youth's throbbing pulse is bounding,
Fann'd by the magic breath your march surrounding.

Shades fondly loved appear, your train attending,
And visions fair of many a blissful day;
First-love and friendship their fond accents blending,
Like to some ancient, half-expiring lay;
Sorrow revives, her wail of anguish sending
Back o'er life's devious labyrinthine way,
And names the dear ones, they whom Fate bereaving
Of life's fair hours, left me behind them grieving.

They hear me not my later cadence singing,
The souls to whom my earlier lays I sang;
Dispersed the throng, their severed flight now winging;
Mute are the voices that responsive rang.
For stranger crowds the Orphean lyre now stringing,
E'en their applause is to my heart a pang;
Of old who listened to my song, glad hearted,
If yet they live, now wander widely parted.

A yearning long unfelt, each impulse swaying,
To yon calm spirit-realm uplifts my soul;
In faltering cadence, as when Zephyr playing,
Fans the Æolian harp, my numbers roll;
Tear follows tear, my steadfast heart obeying
The tender impulse, loses its control;
What I possess as from afar I see;
Those I have lost become realities to me.

DRAMATIS PERSONAE

The Manager.
The Dramatic Poet. } Characters in the Prologue
Merryman.   for the Theatre.

The Lord.
Raphael.
Gabriel. } The Archangels.   } Characters in the
Michael.   Prologue in Heaven.
(The Heavenly Host)
Mephistopheles.

Faust.
Mephistopheles.
Wagner, a student.
Margaret.
Martha, Margaret's neighbour.
Valentine, Margaret's brother.
Old Peasant.
A Student.
Elizabeth, an acquaintance of Margaret's.

Frosch.
Brander. } Guests in Auerbach's Wine Cellar.
Siebel.
Altmayer.

Witches, old and young, Wizards, Will-o'-the-Wisp, Witch Pedlar, Proctophantasmist, Servibilis, Monkeys, Spirits, Journeymen, Country-folk, Citizens, Beggar, Old Fortune-teller, Shepherd, Soldier, Students, &c.

Oberon.
Titania. } In the Intermezzo.
Ariel.
Puck, &c., &c.

3

PROLOGUE FOR THE THEATRE

MANAGER, DRAMATIC POET, MERRYMAN.

MANAGER. Ye twain, in trouble and distress
      True friends whom I so oft have found,
      Say, for our scheme on German ground,
      What prospect have we of success?
      Fain would I please the public, win their thanks;
      They live and let live, hence it is but meet.
      The posts are now erected, and the planks,
      And all look forward to a festal treat.
      Their places taken, they, with eyebrows rais'd,
      Sit patiently, and fain would be amaz'd.
      I know the art to hit the public taste,
      Yet ne'er of failure felt so keen a dread;
      True, they are not accustomed to the best,
      But then appalling the amount they've read.
      How make our entertainment striking, new,
      And yet significant and pleasing too?
      For to be plain, I love to see the throng,
      As to our booth the living tide progresses;
      As wave on wave successive rolls along,
      And through heaven's narrow portal forceful presses;
      Still in broad daylight, ere the clock strikes four,
      With blows their way towards the box they take;
      And, as for bread in famine, at the baker's door,
      For tickets are content their necks to break.
      Such various minds the bard alone can sway,
      My friend, oh work this miracle to-day!
POET.   Oh of the motley throng speak not before me,
      At whose aspect the Spirit wings its flight!
      Conceal the surging concourse, I implore thee,
      Whose vortex draws us with resistless might.
      No, to some peaceful heavenly nook restore me,
      Where only for the bard blooms pure delight,
      Where love and friendship yield their choicest blessing,
      Our heart's true bliss, with god-like hand caressing.

5

What in the spirit's depths was there created,
What shyly there the lip shaped forth in sound;
A failure now, with words now fitly mated,
In the wild tumult of the hour is drown'd;
Full oft the poet's thought for years hath waited
Until at length with perfect form 'tis crowned;
What dazzles, for the moment born, must perish;
What genuine is posterity will cherish.

MERRYMAN.   This cant about posterity I hate;
About posterity were I to prate,
Who then the living would amuse? For they
Will have diversion, ay, and 'tis their due.
A sprightly fellow's presence at your play,
Methinks should also count for something too;
Whose genial wit the audience still inspires,
Knows from their changeful mood no angry feeling;
A wider circle he desires,
To their heart's depths more surely thus appealing.
To work, then! Give a master-piece, my friend;
Bring Fancy with her choral trains before us,
Sense, reason, feeling, passion, but attend!
Let folly also swell the tragic chorus.

MANAGER.   In chief, of incident enough prepare!
A show they want, they come to gape and stare.
Spin for their eyes abundant occupation,
So that the multitude may wondering gaze,
You by sheer bulk have won your reputation,
The man you are all love to praise.
By mass alone can you subdue the masses,
Each then selects in time what suits his bent.
Bring much, you something bring for various classes,
And from the house goes every one content.
You give a piece, abroad in pieces send it!
'Tis a ragout—success must needs attend it;
'Tis easy to serve up, as easy to invent.
A finish'd whole what boots it to present!
Full soon the public will in pieces rend it.

POET.   How mean such handicraft as this you cannot feel!
How it revolts the genuine artist's mind!
The sorry trash in which these coxcombs deal,
Is here approved on principle, I find.

MANAGER.   Such a reproof disturbs me not a whit!
   Who on efficient work is bent,
   Must choose the fittest instrument.
   Consider! 'tis soft wood you have to split;
   Think too for whom you write, I pray!
   One comes to while an hour away;
   One from the festive board, a sated guest;
   Others, more dreaded than the rest,
   From journal-reading hurry to the play.
   As to a masquerade, with absent minds, they press,
   Sheer curiosity their footsteps winging;
   Ladies display their persons and their dress,
   Actors unpaid their service bringing.
   What dreams beguile you on your poet's height?
   What puts a full house in a merry mood?
   More closely view your patrons of the night!
   The half are cold, the half are rude.
   One, the play over, craves a game of cards;
   Another a wild night in wanton joy would spend.
   Poor fools the muses' fair regards.
   Why court for such a paltry end?
   I tell you, give them more, still more, 'tis all I ask,
   Thus you will ne'er stray widely from the goal;
   Your audience seek to mystify, cajole; —
   To satisfy them — that's a harder task.
   What ails thee? art enraptured or distressed?
POET.   Depart! elsewhere another servant choose;
   What! shall the bard his godlike power abuse?
   Man's loftiest right, kind nature's high bequest,
   For your mean purpose basely sport away?
   Whence comes his mastery o'er the human breast,
   Whence o'er the elements his sway,
   But from the harmony that, gushing from his soul,
   Draws back into his heart the wondrous whole?
   With careless hand when round her spindle, Nature
   Winds the interminable thread of life;
   When 'mid the clash of Being every creature
   Mingles in harsh inextricable strife;
   Who deals their course unvaried till it falleth,
   In rhythmic flow to music's measur'd tone?
   Each solitary note whose genius calleth,

To swell the mighty choir in unison?
Who in the raging storm sees passion low'ring?
Or flush of earnest thought in evening's glow?
Who every blossom in sweet spring-time flowering
Along the loved one's path would strow?
Who, Nature's green familiar leaves entwining,
Wreathes glory's garland, won on every field?
Makes sure Olympus, heavenly powers combining?
Man's mighty spirit, in the bard reveal'd!

MERRYMAN.   Come then, employ your lofty inspiration,
And carry on the poet's avocation,
Just as we carry on a love affair.
Two meet by chance, are pleased, they linger there,
Insensibly are link'd, they scarce know how;
Fortune seems now propitious, adverse now,
Then come alternate rapture and despair;
And 'tis a true romance ere one's aware.
Just such a drama let us now compose.
Plunge boldly into life — its depths disclose!
Each lives it, not to many is it known,
'Twill interest wheresoever seiz'd and shown;
Bright pictures, but obscure their meaning:
A ray of truth through error gleaming,
Thus you the best elixir brew,
To charm mankind, and edify them too.
Then youth's fair blossoms crowd to view your play,
And wait as on an oracle; while they,
The tender souls, who love the melting mood,
Suck from your work their melancholy food;
Now this one, and now that, you deeply stir,
Each sees the working of his heart laid bare.
Their tears, their laughter, you command with ease,
The lofty still they honour, the illusive love.
Your finish'd gentlemen you ne'er can please;
A growing mind alone will grateful prove.

POET.   Then give me back youth's golden prime,
When my own spirit too was growing,
When from my heart th' unbidden rhyme
Gush'd forth, a fount for ever flowing;
Then shadowy mist the world conceal'd,
And every bud sweet promise made,

Of wonders yet to be reveal'd,
As through the vales, with blooms inlaid,
Culling a thousand flowers I stray'd.
Naught had I, yet a rich profusion!
The thirst for truth, joy in each fond illusion.
Give me unquell'd those impulses to prove; —
Rapture so deep, its ecstasy was pain,
The power of hate, the energy of love,
Give me, oh give me back my youth again!

MERRYMAN.   Youth, my good friend, you certainly require
When foes in battle round are pressing,
When a fair maid, her heart on fire,
Hangs on your neck with fond caressing,
When from afar, the victor's crown,
To reach the hard-won goal inciteth;
When from the whirling dance, to drown
Your sense, the night's carouse inviteth.
But the familiar chords among
Boldly to sweep, with graceful cunning,
While to its goal, the verse along
Its winding path is sweetly running;
This task is yours, old gentlemen, to-day;
Nor are you therefore less in reverence held;
Age does not make us childish, as folk say,
It finds us genuine children e'en in eld.[1]

MANAGER.   A truce to words, mere empty sound,
Let deeds at length appear, my friends!
While idle compliments you round,
You might achieve some useful ends.
Why talk of the poetic vein?
Who hesitates will never know it;
If bards ye are, as ye maintain,
Now let your inspiration show it.
To you is known what we require,
Strong drink to sip is our desire;
Come, brew me such without delay!
To-morrow sees undone, what happens not to-day;
Still forward press, nor ever tire!
The possible, with steadfast trust,

---

1. *eld*] old age.

Resolve should by the forelock grasp;
Then she will ne'er let go her clasp,
And labours on, because she must.

On German boards, you're well aware,
The taste of each may have full sway;
Therefore in bringing out your play,
Nor scenes nor mechanism spare!
Heaven's lamps employ, the greatest and the least,
Be lavish of the stellar lights,
Water, and fire, and rocky heights,
Spare not at all, nor birds, nor beast.
Thus let creation's ample sphere
Forthwith in this our narrow booth appear,
And with considerate speed, through fancy's spell,
Journey from heaven, thence through the world, to hell!

PROLOGUE IN HEAVEN

THE LORD, THE HEAVENLY HOSTS, *afterwards* MEPHISTOPHELES.

The three Archangels come forward.

RAPHAEL.   The Sun, in ancient guise, competing
    With brother spheres in rival song,
    With thunder-march, his orb completing,
    Moves his predestin'd course along;
    His aspect to the powers supernal
    Gives strength, though fathom him none may;
    Transcending thought, the works eternal
    Are fair as on the primal day.

GABRIEL.   With speed, thought baffling, unabating,
    Earth's splendour whirls in circling flight;
    Its Eden-brightness alternating
    With solemn, awe-inspiring night;
    Ocean's broad waves in wild commotion,
    Against the rocks' deep base are hurled;
    And with the spheres, both rock and ocean
    Eternally are swiftly whirled.

MICHAEL.   And tempests roar in emulation
    From sea to land, from land to sea,
    And raging form, without cessation,
    A chain of wondrous agency,
    Full in the thunder's path careering,
    Flaring the swift destructions play;
    But, Lord, thy servants are revering
    The mild procession of thy day.

THE THREE.   Thine aspect to the powers supernal
    Gives strength, though fathom thee none may;
    And all thy works, sublime, eternal,
    Are fair as on the primal day.

MEPH.   Since thou, O Lord, approachest us once more,
    And how it fares with us, to ask art fain,
    Since thou hast kindly welcom'd me of yore,
    Thou see'st me also now among thy train.
    Excuse me, fine harangues I cannot make,
    Though all the circle look on me with scorn;

My pathos soon thy laughter would awake,
Hadst thou the laughing mood not long forsworn.
Of suns and worlds I nothing have to say,
I see alone mankind's self-torturing pains.
The little world-god still the self-same stamp retains,
And is as wondrous now as on the primal day.
Better he might have fared, poor wight,
Hadst thou not given him a gleam of heavenly light;
Reason, he names it, and doth so
Use it, than brutes more brutish still to grow.
With deference to your grace, he seems to me
Like any long-legged grasshopper to be,
Which ever flies, and flying springs,
And in the grass its ancient ditty sings.
Would he but always in the grass repose!
In every heap of dung he thrusts his nose.

THE LORD.   Hast thou naught else to say? Is blame
In coming here, as ever, thy sole aim?
Does nothing on the earth to thee seem right?

MEPH.   No, Lord! I find things there, as ever, in sad plight.
Men, in their evil days, move my compassion;
Such sorry things to plague is nothing worth.

THE LORD.   Know'st thou my servant, Faust?

MEPH.   The doctor?

THE LORD.   Right.

MEPH.   He serves thee truly in a wondrous fashion.
Poor fool! His food and drink are not of earth.
An inward impulse hurries him afar,
Himself half conscious of his frenzied mood;
From heaven claimeth he the fairest star,
And from the earth craves every highest good,
And all that's near, and all that's far,
Fails to allay the tumult in his blood.

THE LORD.   Though in perplexity he serves me now,
I soon will lead him where more light appears;
When buds the sapling, doth the gardener know
That flowers and fruit will deck the coming years.

MEPH.   What wilt thou wager? Him thou yet shall lose,
If leave to me thou wilt but give,
Gently to lead him as I choose!

THE LORD.   So long as he on earth doth live,

So long 'tis not forbidden thee.
Man still must err, while he doth strive.

MEPH.   I thank you; for not willingly
I traffic with the dead, and still aver
That youth's plump blooming cheek I very much prefer.
I'm not at home to corpses; 'tis my way,
Like cats with captive mice to toy and play.

THE LORD.   Enough! 'tis granted thee! Divert
This mortal spirit from his primal source;
Him, canst thou seize, thy power exert
And lead him on thy downward course,
Then stand abash'd, when thou perforce must own,
A good man in his darkest aberration,
Of the right path is conscious still.

MEPH.   'Tis done! Full soon thou'lt see my exultation;
As for my bet no fears I entertain.
And if my end I finally should gain,
Excuse my triumphing with all my soul.
Dust he shall eat, ay, and with relish take,
As did my cousin, the renownèd snake.

THE LORD.   Here too thou'rt free to act without control;
I ne'er have cherished hate for such as thee.
Of all the spirits who deny,
The scoffer is least wearisome to me.
Ever too prone is man activity to shirk,
In unconditioned rest he fain would live;
Hence this companion purposely I give,
Who stirs, excites, and must, as devil, work.
But ye, the genuine sons of heaven, rejoice!
In the full living beauty still rejoice!
May that which works and lives, the ever-growing,
In bonds of love enfold you, mercy-fraught,
And Seeming's changeful forms, around you flowing,
Do ye arrest, in ever-during thought!

[*Heaven closes, the Archangels disperse.*]

MEPH.   [*Alone*] The ancient one I like sometimes to see,
And not to break with him am always civil;
'Tis courteous in so great a lord as he,
To speak so kindly even to the devil.

SCENE — *Night* — *A high vaulted narrow Gothic chamber*

FAUST, *restless, seated at his desk.*

FAUST.   I have, alas! Philosophy,
    Medicine, Jurisprudence too,
    And to my cost Theology,
    With ardent labour, studied through.
    And here I stand, with all my lore,
    Poor fool, no wiser than before.
    Magister,[1] doctor styled, indeed,
    Already these ten years I lead,
    Up, down, across, and to and fro,
    My pupils by the nose, — and learn,
    That we in truth can nothing know!
    That in my heart like fire doth burn.
    'Tis true I've more cunning than all your dull tribe,
    Magister and doctor, priest, parson, and scribe;
    Scruple or doubt comes not to enthrall me,
    Neither can devil nor hell now appal me —
    Hence also my heart must all pleasure forego!
    I may not pretend, aught rightly to know,
    I may not pretend, through teaching, to find
    A means to improve or convert mankind.
    Then I have neither goods nor treasure,
    No worldly honour, rank, or pleasure;
    No dog in such fashion would longer live!
    Therefore myself to magic I give,
    In hope, through spirit-voice and might,
    Secrets now veiled to bring to light,
    That I no more, with aching brow,
    Need speak of what I nothing know;
    That I the force may recognise
    That binds creation's inmost energies;

---

1. *Magister*] Master; a medieval title, given to a person in authority, or to one having an academic license to teach.

Her vital powers, her embryo seeds survey,
And fling the trade in empty words away.
O full-orb'd moon, did but thy rays
Their last upon mine anguish gaze!
Beside this desk, at dead of night,
Oft have I watched to hail thy light:
Then, pensive friend! o'er book and scroll,
With soothing power, thy radiance stole!
In thy dear light, ah, might I climb,
Freely, some mountain height sublime,
Round mountain caves with spirits ride,
In thy mild haze o'er meadows glide,
And, purged from knowledge-fumes, renew
My spirit, in thy healing dew!
Woe's me! still prison'd in the gloom
Of this abhorr'd and musty room!
Where heaven's dear light itself doth pass,
But dimly through the painted glass!
Hemmed in by volumes thick with dust,
Worm-eaten, hid 'neath rust and mould,
And to the high vault's topmost bound,
A smoke-stained paper compassed round;
With boxes round thee piled, and glass,
And many a useless instrument,
With old ancestral lumber blent—
This is thy world! a world! alas!
And dost thou ask why heaves thy heart,
With tighten'd pressure in thy breast?
Why the dull ache will not depart,
By which thy life-pulse is oppress'd?
Instead of nature's living sphere,
Created for mankind of old,
Brute skeletons surround thee here,
And dead men's bones in smoke and mould.

Up! Forth into the distant land!
Is not this book of mystery
By Nostradamus' [2] proper hand,

2. *Nostradamus*] sixteenth-century physician and astrologer, some of whose prophecies
appeared to be fulfilled during his lifetime; in 1781 the Roman Catholic Church
condemned his book of prophecies, *Centuries*, which still generates controversy.

An all-sufficient guide? Thou'lt see
The courses of the stars unroll'd;
When nature doth her thoughts unfold
To thee, thy soul shall rise, and seek
Communion high with her to hold,
As spirit doth with spirit speak!
Vain by dull poring to divine
The meaning of each hallow'd sign.
Spirits! I feel you hov'ring near;
Make answer, if my voice ye hear!

[*He opens the book and perceives the sign of the Macro-cosmos.*]

Ah! at this spectacle through every sense,
What sudden ecstasy of joy is flowing!
I feel new rapture, hallow'd and intense,
Through every nerve and vein with ardour glowing.
Was it a god who character'd this scroll,
The tumult in my spirit healing,
O'er my sad heart with rapture stealing,
And by a mystic impulse, to my soul,
The powers of nature all around revealing.
Am I a God? What light intense!
In these pure symbols do I see,
Nature exert her vital energy.
Now of the wise man's words I learn the sense;

> "Unlock'd the spirit-world doth lie,
>   Thy sense is shut, thy heart is dead!
>   Up scholar, lave, with courage high,
>   Thine earthly breast in the morning-red!"

[*He contemplates the sign.*]

How all things live and work, and ever blending,
Weave one vast whole from Being's ample range!
How powers celestial, rising and descending,
Their golden buckets ceaseless interchange!
Their flight on rapture-breathing pinions winging,
From heaven to earth their genial influence bringing,
Through the wild sphere their chimes melodious ringing!

A wondrous show! but ah! a show alone!
Where shall I grasp thee, infinite nature, where?

Ye breasts, ye fountains of all life, whereon
Hang heaven and earth, from which the withered heart
For solace yearns, ye still impart
Your sweet and fostering tides — where are ye — where?
Ye gush, and must I languish in despair?

[*He turns over the leaves of the book impatiently, and perceives
the sign of the Earth-spirit.*]

How all unlike the influence of this sign!
Earth-spirit, thou to me art nigher,
E'en now my strength is rising higher,
E'en now I glow as with new wine;
Courage I feel, abroad the world to dare,
The woe of earth, the bliss of earth to bear,
With storms to wrestle, brave the lightning's glare,
And mid the crashing shipwreck not despair.

Clouds gather over me —
The moon conceals her light —
The lamp is quench'd —
Vapours are rising — Quiv'ring round my head
Flash the red beams — Down from the vaulted roof
A shuddering horror floats,
And seizes me!
I feel it, spirit, prayer-compell'd, 'tis thou
Art hovering near!
Unveil thyself!
Ha! How my heart is riven now!
Each sense, with eager palpitation,
Is strain'd to catch some new sensation!
I feel my heart surrender'd unto thee!
Thou must! Thou must! Though life should be the fee!

[*He seizes the book, and pronounces mysteriously the sign of the spirit. A
ruddy flame flashes up; the spirit appears in the flame.*]

SPIRIT.   Who calls me?
FAUST.   [*Turning aside*] Dreadful shape!
SPIRIT.   With might,
Thou hast compelled me to appear,
Long hast been sucking at my sphere,
And now —

FAUST.   Woe's me! I cannot bear thy sight!
SPIRIT.   To see me thou dost breathe thine invocation,
     My voice to hear, to gaze upon my brow;
     Me doth thy strong entreaty bow —
     Lo! I am here! — What cowering agitation
     Grasps thee, the demigod! Where's now the soul's deep cry?
     Where is the breast, which in its depths a world conceiv'd
     And bore and cherished? which, with ecstasy,
     To rank itself with us, the spirits, heaved?
     Where art thou, Faust? whose voice I heard resound,
     Who towards me press'd with energy profound?
     Art thou he? Thou, — who by my breath art blighted,
     Who, in his spirit's depths affrighted,
     Trembles, a crush'd and writhing worm!
FAUST.   Shall I yield, thing of flame, to thee?
     Faust, and thine equal, I am he!
SPIRIT.   In the currents of life, in action's storm,
                    I float and I wave
                    With billowy motion!
                    Birth and the grave
                    A limitless ocean,
                    A constant weaving
                    With change still rife,
                    A restless heaving,
                    A glowing life —
     Thus time's whirring loom unceasing I ply,
     And weave the life-garment of deity.
FAUST.   Thou, restless spirit, dost from end to end
     O'ersweep the world; how near I feel to thee!
SPIRIT.   Thou'rt like the spirit, thou dost comprehend,
     Not me!   [Vanishes.]
FAUST.   [Deeply moved] Not thee?
     Whom then?
     I, God's own image!
     And not rank with thee!   [A knock.]
     Oh death! I know it — 'tis my famulus[3] —
     My fairest fortune now escapes!

---

3. *famulus*] professor's assistant; private secretary, attendant.

That all these visionary shapes
A soulless groveller should banish thus!

[WAGNER *in his dressing gown and night-cap, a lamp in his
hand.* FAUST *turns round reluctantly.*]

WAGNER.   Pardon! I heard you here declaim;
A Grecian tragedy you doubtless read?
Improvement in this art is now my aim,
For now-a-days it much avails. Indeed
An actor, oft I've heard it said, as teacher,
May give instruction to a preacher.
FAUST.   Ay, if your priest should be an actor too,
As not improbably may come to pass.
WAGNER.   When in his study pent the whole year through,
Man views the world, as through an optic glass,
On a chance holiday, and scarcely then,
How by persuasion can he govern men?
FAUST.   If feeling prompt not, if it doth not flow
Fresh from the spirit's depths, with strong control
Swaying to rapture every listener's soul,
Idle your toil; the chase you may forego!
Brood o'er your task! Together glue,
Cook from another's feast your own ragout,
Still prosecute your paltry game,
And fan your ash-heaps into flame!
Thus children's wonder you'll excite,
And apes', if such your appetite;
But that which issues from the heart alone,
Will bend the hearts of others to your own.
WAGNER.   The speaker in delivery will find
Success alone; I still am far behind.
FAUST.   A worthy object still pursue!
Be not a hollow tinkling fool!
Sound understanding, judgment true,
Find utterance without art or rule;
And when in earnest you are moved to speak,
Then is it needful cunning words to seek?
Your fine harangues, so polish'd in their kind,
Wherein the shreds of human thought ye twist,
Are unrefreshing as the empty wind,
Whistling through wither'd leaves and autumn mist!

WAGNER.   Oh God! How long is art,
       Our life how short! With earnest zeal
       Still as I ply the critic's task, I feel
       A strange oppression both of head and heart.
       The very means how hardly are they won,
       By which wc to thc fountains rise!
       And haply, ere one half the course is run,
       Check'd in his progress, the poor devil dies.
FAUST.   Parchment, is that the sacred fount whence roll
       Waters, he thirsteth not who once hath quaffed?
       Oh, if it gush not from thine inmost soul,
       Thou has not won the life-restoring draught.
WAGNER.   Your pardon! 'tis delightful to transport
       Oneself into the spirit of the past,
       To see in times before us how a wise man thought,
       And what a glorious height we have achieved at last.
FAUST.   Ay truly! even to the loftiest star!
       To us, my friend, the ages that are pass'd
       A book with seven seals, close-fasten'd, are;
       And what the spirit of the times men call,
       Is merely their own spirit after all,
       Wherein, distorted oft, the times are glass'd.
       Then truly, 'tis a sight to grieve the soul!
       At the first glance we fly it in dismay;
       A very lumber-room, a rubbish-hole;
       At best a sort of mock-heroic play,
       With saws pragmatical, and maxims sage,
       To suit the puppets and their mimic stage.
WAGNER.   But then the world and man, his heart and brain!
       Touching these things all men would something know.
FAUST.   Ay! what 'mong men as knowledge doth obtain!
       Who on the child its true name dares bestow?
       The few who somewhat of these things have known,
       Who their full hearts unguardedly reveal'd,
       Nor thoughts, nor feelings, from the mob conceal'd,
       Have died on crosses, or in flames been thrown. —
       Excuse me, friend, far now the night is spent,
       For this time we must say adieu.
WAGNER.   Still to watch on I had been well content,
       Thus to converse so learnedly with you.
       But as to-morrow will be Easter-day,

Some further questions grant, I pray;
With diligence to study still I fondly cling;
Already I know much, but would know every thing.   [*Exit.*]

FAUST.   [*Alone*] How him alone all hope abandons never,
To empty trash who clings, with zeal untired,
With greed for treasure gropes, and, joy-inspir'd,
Exults if earth-worms second his endeavour.

And dare a voice of merely human birth,
E'en here, where shapes immortal throng'd, intrude?
Yet ah! thou poorest of the sons of earth,
For once, I e'en to thee feel gratitude.
Despair the power of sense did well-nigh blast,
And thou didst save me ere I sank dismay'd,
So giant-like the vision seem'd, so vast,
I felt myself shrink dwarf'd as I survey'd!

I, God's own image, from this toil of clay
Already freed, with eager joy who hail'd
The mirror of eternal truth unveil'd,
Mid light effulgent and celestial day: —
I, more than·cherub, whose unfetter'd soul
With penetrative glance aspir'd to flow
Through nature's veins, and, still creating, know
The life of gods, — how am I punish'd now!
One thunder-word hath hurl'd me from the goal!

Spirit! I dare not lift me to thy sphere.
What though my power compell'd thee to appear,
My art was powerless to detain thee here.
In that great moment, rapture-fraught,
I felt myself so small, so great;
Fiercely didst thrust me from the realm of thought
Back on humanity's uncertain fate!
Who'll teach me now? What ought I to forego?
Ought I that impulse to obey?
Alas! our every deed, as well as every woe,
Impedes the tenor of life's onward way!

E'en to the noblest by the soul conceiv'd,
Some feelings cling of baser quality;
And when the goods of this world are achiev'd,

Each nobler aim is termed a cheat, a lie.
Our aspirations, our soul's genuine life,
Grow torpid in the din of earthly strife.
Though youthful phantasy, while hope inspires,
Stretch o'er the infinite her wing sublime,
A narrow compass limits her desires,
When wreck'd our fortunes in the gulf of time.
In the deep heart of man care builds her nest,
O'er secret woes she broodeth there,
Sleepless she rocks herself and scareth joy and rest;
Still is she wont some new disguise to wear,
She may as house and court, as wife and child appear,
As dagger, poison, fire and flood;
Imagined evils chill thy blood,

      And what thou ne'er shall lose, o'er that dost shed the tear.
      I am not like the gods! Feel it I must;
      I'm like the earth-worm, writhing in the dust,
      Which, as on dust it feeds, its native fare,
      Crushed 'neath the passer's tread, lies buried there.

Is it not dust, wherewith this lofty wall,
With hundred shelves, confines me round;
Rubbish, in thousand shapes, may I not call
What in this moth-world doth my being bound?
Here, what doth fail me, shall I find?
Read in a thousand tomes that, everywhere,
Self-torture is the lot of human-kind,
With but one mortal happy, here and there?
Thou hollow skull, that grin, what should it say,
But that thy brain, like mine, of old perplexed,
Still yearning for the truth, hath sought the light of day.
And in the twilight wandered, sorely vexed?
Ye instruments, forsooth, ye mock at me, —
With wheel, and cog, and ring, and cylinder;
To nature's portals ye should be the key;
Cunning your wards, and yet the bolts ye fail to stir.
Inscrutable in broadest light,
To be unveil'd by force she doth refuse,
What she reveals not to thy mental sight,
Thou wilt not wrest me from her with levers and with screws.

Old useless furnitures, yet stand ye here,
Because my sire ye served, now dead and gone.
Old scroll, the smoke of years dost wear,
So long as o'er this desk the sorry lamp hath shone.
Better my little means hath squandered quite away,
Than burden'd by that little here to sweat and groan!
Wouldst thou possess thy heritage, essay,
By use to render it thine own!
What we employ not, but impedes our way,
That which the hour creates, that can it use alone!
But wherefore to yon spot is riveted my gaze?
Is yonder flasket there a magnet to my sight?
Whence this mild radiance that around me plays,
As when, 'mid forest gloom, reigneth the moon's soft light?

Hail precious phial! Thee, with reverent awe,
Down from thine old receptacle I draw!
Science in thee I hail and human art.
Essence of deadliest powers, refin'd and sure,
Of soothing anodynes abstraction pure,
Now in thy master's need thy grace impart!
I gaze on thee, my pain is lull'd to rest;
I grasp thee, calm'd the tumult in my breast;
The flood-tide of my spirit ebbs away;
Onward I'm summon'd o'er a boundless main,
Calm at my feet expands the glassy plain,
To shores unknown allures a brighter day.

Lo, where a car of fire, on airy pinion,
Comes floating towards me! I'm prepar'd to fly
By a new track through ether's wide dominion,
To distant spheres of pure activity.
This life intense, this godlike ecstasy —
Worm that thou art such rapture canst thou earn?
Only resolve with courage stern and high,
Thy visage from the radiant sun to turn!
Dare with determin'd will to burst the portals
Past which in terror others fain would steal!
Now is the time, through deeds, to show that mortals
The calm sublimity of gods can feel;
To shudder not at yonder dark abyss,
Where phantasy creates her own self-torturing brood,

Right onward to the yawning gulf to press,
Around whose narrow jaws rolleth hell's fiery flood;
With glad resolve to take the fatal leap,
Though danger threaten thee, to sink in endless sleep!
Pure crystal goblet! forth I draw thee now,
From out thine antiquated case, where thou
Forgotten hast reposed for many a year!
Oft at my father's revels thou didst shine,
To glad the earnest guests was thine,
As each to other passed the generous cheer.
The gorgeous brede[4] of figures, quaintly wrought,
Which he who quaff'd must first in rhyme expound,
Then drain the goblet at one draught profound,
Hath nights of boyhood to fond memory brought.
I to my neighbour shall not reach thee now,
Nor on thy rich device shall I my cunning show.
Here is a juice, makes drunk without delay;
Its dark brown flood thy crystal round doth fill;
Let this last draught, the product of my skill,
My own free choice, be quaff'd with resolute will,
A solemn festive greeting, to the coming day!

> [*He places the goblet to his mouth.*]
> [*The ringing of bells, and choral voices.*]

CHORUS OF ANGELS

> Christ is arisen!
> Mortal, all hail to thee,
> Thou whom mortality,
> Earth's sad reality,
> Held as in prison.

FAUST.   What hum melodious, what clear silvery chime
Thus draws the goblet from my lips away?
Ye deep-ton'd bells, do ye with voice sublime,
Announce the solemn dawn of Easter-day?
Sweet choir! are ye the hymn of comfort singing,
Which once around the darkness of the grave,
From seraph-voices, in glad triumph ringing,
Of a new covenant assurance gave?

4. *brede*] embroidery.

Chorus of Women

We, his true-hearted,
With spices and myrrh,
Embalmed the departed,
And swathed him with care;
Here we conveyed Him,
Our Master, so dear;
Alas! Where we laid Him,
The Christ is not here.

Chorus of Angels

Christ is arisen!
Blessèd the loving one,
Who from earth's trial throes,
Healing and strengthening woes,
Soars as from prison.

FAUST.   Wherefore, ye tones celestial, sweet and strong,
Come ye a dweller in the dust to seek?
Ring out your chimes believing crowds among,
The message well I hear, my faith alone is weak;
From faith her darling, miracle, hath sprung.
Aloft to yonder spheres I dare not soar,
Whence sound the tidings of great joy;
And yet, with this sweet strain familiar when a boy,
Back it recalleth me to life once more.
Then would celestial love, with holy kiss,
Come o'er me in the Sabbath's stilly hour,
While, fraught with solemn meaning and mysterious power,
Chim'd the deep-sounding bell, and prayer was bliss;
A yearning impulse, undefin'd yet dear,
Drove me to wander on through wood and field;
With heaving breast and many a burning tear,
I felt with holy joy a world reveal'd.
Gay sports and festive hours proclaim'd with joyous pealing,
This Easter hymn in days of old;
And fond remembrance now doth me, with childlike feeling,
Back from the last, the solemn step, withhold.
O still sound on, thou sweet celestial strain!
The tear-drop flows, — Earth, I am thine again!

CHORUS OF DISCIPLES

He whom we mourned as dead,
Living and glorious,
From the dark grave hath fled,
O'er death victorious;
Almost creative bliss
Waits on his growing powers;
Ah! Him on earth we miss;
Sorrow and grief are ours.
Yearning he left his own,
Mid sore annoy;
Ah! we must needs bemoan.
Master, thy joy!

CHORUS OF ANGELS

Christ is arisen,
Redeem'd from decay.
The bonds which imprison
Your souls, rend away!
Praising the Lord with zeal,
By deeds that love reveal,
Like brethren true and leal
Sharing the daily meal,
To all that sorrow feel
Whisp'ring of heaven's weal,
Still is the master near,
Still is he here!

SCENE — *Before the Gate*

Promenaders of all sorts pass out. FAUST, WAGNER.

ARTISANS.   Why choose ye that direction, pray?
OTHERS.   To the hunting-lodge we're on our way.
THE FIRST.   We towards the mill are strolling on.
A MECHANIC.   A walk to Wasserhof were best.
A SECOND.   The road is not a pleasant one.
OTHERS.   What will you do?
A THIRD.   I'll join the rest.

A FOURTH.   Let's up to Burghof, there you'll find good cheer,
      The prettiest maidens and the best of beer,
      And brawls of a prime sort.
A FIFTH.   You scapegrace! How;
      Your skin still itching for a row?
      Thither I will not go, I loathe the place.
SERVANT GIRL.   No, no! I to the town my steps retrace.
ANOTHER.   Near yonder poplars he is sure to be.
THE FIRST.   And if he is, what matters it to me!
      With you he'll walk, he'll dance with none but you,
      And with your pleasures what have I to do?
THE SECOND.   To-day he will not be alone, he said
      His friend would be with him, the curly-head.
STUDENT.   Why how those buxom girls step on!
      Come, brother, we will follow them anon.
      Strong beer, a damsel smartly dress'd,
      Stinging tobacco, — these I love the best.
BURGHER'S DAUGHTER.   Look at those handsome fellows there!
      'Tis really shameful, I declare,
      The very best society they shun,
      After those servant girls forsooth, to run.
SECOND STUDENT.   [*To the first*] Not quite so fast! for in our rear,
      Two girls, well-dress'd, are drawing near;
      Not far from us the one doth dwell,
      And sooth to say, I like her well.
      They walk demurely, yet you'll see,
      That they will let us join them presently.
THE FIRST.   Not I! restraints of all kinds I detest.
      Quick! let us catch the wild-game ere it flies,
      The hand on Saturday the mop that plies,
      Will on the Sunday fondle you the best.
BURGHER.   No, this new Burgomaster, I like him not, God knows,
      Now, he's in office, daily more arrogant he grows;
      And for the town, what doth he do for it?
      Are not things worse from day to day?
      To more restraints we must submit;
      And taxes more than ever pay.
BEGGAR.
                    [*Sings*]
            Kind gentlemen and ladies fair,
            So rosy-cheek'd and trimly dress'd,

Be pleas'd to listen to my prayer,
Relieve and pity the distress'd.
Let me not vainly sing my lay!
His heart's most glad whose hand is free.
Now when all men keep holiday,
Should be a harvest-day to me.

ANOTHER BURGHER.   On holidays and Sundays naught know I more
   inviting
Than chatting about war and war's alarms,
When folk in Turkey, up in arms,
Far off, are 'gainst each other fighting.
We at the window stand, our glasses drain,
2And watch adown the stream the painted vessels gliding,
Then joyful we at eve come home again,
And peaceful times we bless, peace long-abiding.
THIRD BURGHER.   Ay, neighbour! So let matters stand for me!
There they may scatter one another's brains,
And wild confusion round them see —
So here at home in quiet all remains!
OLD WOMAN.   [To the BURGHERS' DAUGHTERS] Heyday! How smart!
   The fresh young blood!
Who would not fall in love with you?
Not quite so proud! 'Tis well and good!
And what you wish, that I could help you to.
BURGHER'S DAUGHTER.   Come, Agatha! I care not to be seen
Walking in public with these witches. True,
My future lover, last St. Andrew's E'en,
In flesh and blood she brought before my view.
ANOTHER.   And mine she show'd me also in the glass,
A soldier's figure, with companions bold;
I look around, I seek him as I pass,
In vain, his form I nowhere can behold.
SOLDIERS.   Fortress with turrets
              And walls high in air,
              Damsel disdainful,
              Haughty and fair,
              These be my prey!
              Bold is the venture,
              Costly the pay!

              Hark how the trumpet

Thither doth call us,
Where either pleasure
Or death may befall us.
Hail to the tumult!
Life's in the field!
Damsel and fortress
To us must yield.
Bold is the venture,
Costly the pay!
Gaily the soldier
Marches away.

FAUST, WAGNER.

FAUST.   Loosed from their fetters are streams and rills
Through the gracious spring-tide's all-quickening glow;
Hope's budding joy in the vale doth blow;
Old Winter back to the savage hills
Withdraweth his force, decrepid now.
Thence only impotent icy grains
Scatters he as he wings his flight,
Striping with sleet the verdant plains;
But the sun endureth no trace of white;
Everywhere growth and movement are rife,
All things investing with hues of life:
Though flowers are lacking, varied of dye,
Their colours the motly throng supply.
Turn thee around, and from this height,
Back to the town direct thy sight.
Forth from the hollow, gloomy gate,
Stream forth the masses, in bright array.
Gladly seek they the sun to-day;
The Lord's Resurrection they celebrate:
For they themselves have risen, with joy,
From tenement sordid, from cheerless room,
From bonds of toil, from care and annoy,
From gable and roof's o'er-hanging gloom,
From crowded alley and narrow street,
And from the churches' awe-breathing night,
All now have come forth into the light.
Look, only look, on nimble feet,
Through garden and field how spread the throng,
How o'er the river's ample sheet,

Many a gay wherry glides along;
And see, deep sinking in the tide,
Pushes the last boat now away.
E'en from yon far hill's path-worn side,
Flash the bright hues of garments gay.
Hark! Sounds of village mirth arise;
This is the people's paradise.
Both great and small send up a cheer;
Here am I man, I feel it here.

WAGNER.   Sir Doctor, in a walk with you
There's honour and instruction too;
Yet here alone I care not to resort,
Because I coarseness hate of every sort.
This fiddling, shouting, skittling, I detest;
I hate the tumult of the vulgar throng;
They roar as by the evil one possess'd,
And call it pleasure, call it song.

PEASANTS [*Under the linden-tree*]

Dance and song

The shepherd for the dance was dress'd,
With ribbon, wreath, and coloured vest,
A gallant show displaying.
And round about the linden-tree,
They footed it right merrily.
      Juchhe! Juchhe!
      Juchheisa! Heisa! He!¹
So fiddle-bow was braying.

Our swain amidst the circle press'd,
He push'd a maiden trimly dress'd,
And jogg'd her with his elbow;
The buxom damsel turn'd her head,
"Now that's a stupid trick!" she said,
      Juchhe! Juchhe!
      Juchheisa! Heisa! He!
Don't be so rude, good fellow!

Swift in the circle they advanced,
They danced to right, to left they danced,
And all the skirts were swinging.

1. *Juchhe! ... He!*] Hurray! Hurrah! Hey!

And they grew red, and they grew warm,
Panting, they rested arm in arm,
>   Juchhe! Juchhe!
>   Juchheisa! Heisa! He!
To hip their elbow bringing.

Don't make so free! How many a maid
Has been betroth'd and then betray'd;
And has repented after!
Yet still he flatter'd her aside,
And from the linden, far and wide,
>   Juchhe! Juchhe!
>   Juchheisa! Heisa! He!
Rang fiddle-bow and laughter.

OLD PEASANT.   Doctor, 'tis really kind of you,
To condescend to come this way,
A highly learned man like you,
To join our mirthful throng to-day.
Our fairest cup I offer you,
Which we with sparkling drink have crown'd,
And pledging you, I pray aloud,
That every drop within its round,
While it your present thirst allays,
May swell the number of your days.

FAUST.   I take the cup you kindly reach,
Thanks and prosperity to each!

[*The crowd gather round in a circle.*]

OLD PEASANT.   Ay, truly! 'tis well done, that you
Our festive meeting thus attend;
You, who in evil days of yore,
So often show'd yourself our friend!
Full many a one stands living here,
Who from the fever's deadly blast,
Your father rescu'd, when his skill
The fatal sickness stay'd at last.
A young man then, each house you sought,
Where reign'd the mortal pestilence.
Corpse after corpse was carried forth,
But still unscath'd you issued thence.
Sore then your trials and severe;
The Helper yonder aids the helper here.

ALL.   Heaven bless the trusty friend, and long
  To help the poor his life prolong!
FAUST.   To Him above in homage bend,
  Who prompts the helper and Who help doth send.

           [*He proceeds with* WAGNER.]

WAGNER.   What feelings, great man, must thy breast inspire,
  At homage paid thee by this crowd! Thrice blest
  Who from the gifts by him possessed
  Such benefit can draw! The sire
  Thee to his boy with reverence shows;
  They press around, inquire, advance,
  Hush'd is the fiddle, check'd the dance.
  Where thou dost pass they stand in rows,
  And each aloft his bonnet throws,
  But little fails and they to thee,
  As though the Host came by, would bend the knee.
FAUST.   A few steps further, up to yonder stone!
  Here rest we from our walk. In times long past,
  Absorb'd in thought, here oft I sat alone,
  And disciplin'd myself with prayer and fast.
  Then rich in hope, with faith sincere,
  With sighs, and hands in anguish press'd,
  The end of that sore plague, with many a tear,
  From heaven's dread Lord, I sought to wrest.
  The crowd's applause assumes a scornful tone.
  Oh, could'st thou in my inner being read,
  How little either sire or son,
  Of such renown deserves the meed![2]
  My sire, of good repute, and sombre mood,
  O'er nature's powers and every mystic zone,
  With honest zeal, but methods of his own,
  With toil fantastic loved to brood;
  His time in dark alchemic cell,
  With brother adepts he would spend,
  And there antagonists compel,
  Through numberless receipts[3] to blend.

 2. *meed*] an earned reward or wage.
 3. *receipts*] formulas according to which things are to be taken or combined, or some effect
  is to be produced; recipes.

A ruddy lion there, a suitor bold,
In tepid bath was with the lily wed.
Thence both, while open flames around them roll'd,
Were tortur'd to another bridal bed.
Was then the youthful queen descried
With varied colours in the flask; —
This was our medicine; the patients died,
"Who were restored?" none cared to ask.
With our infernal mixture thus, ere long,
These hills and peaceful vales among,
We rag'd more fiercely than the pest;[4]
Myself the deadly poison did to thousands give;
They pined away, I yet must live,
To hear the reckless murderers blest.

WAGNER.   Why let this thought your soul o'ercast?
Can man do more than with nice skill,
With firm and conscientious will,
Practise the art transmitted from the past?
If thou thy sire dost honour in thy youth,
His lore thou gladly wilt receive;
In manhood, dost thou spread the bounds of truth,
Then may thy son a higher goal achieve.

FAUST.   How blest, in whom the fond desire
From error's sea to rise, hope still renews!
What a man knows not, that he doth require,
And what he knoweth, that he cannot use.
But let not moody thoughts their shadow throw
O'er the calm beauty of this hour serene!
In the rich sunset see how brightly glow
Yon cottage homes, girt round with verdant green!
Slow sinks the orb, the day is now no more;
Yonder he hastens to diffuse new life.
Oh for a pinion from the earth to soar,
And after, ever after him to strive!
Then should I see the world below,
Bathed in the deathless evening-beams,
The vales reposing, every height a-glow,
The silver brooklets meeting golden streams.
The savage mountain, with its cavern'd side,

---

4. *pest*] pestilence; the plague.

Bars not my godlike progress. Lo, the ocean,
Its warm bays heaving with a tranquil motion,
To my rapt vision opes its ample tide!
But now at length the god appears to sink;
A new-born impulse wings my flight,
Onward I press, his quenchless light to drink,
The day before me, and behind the night,
The pathless waves beneath, and over me the skies.
Fair dream, it vanish'd with the parting day!
Alas! that when on spirit-wing we rise,
No wing material lifts our mortal clay.
But 'tis our inborn impulse, deep and strong,
Upwards and onwards still to urge our flight,
When far above us pours its thrilling song
The sky-lark, lost in azure light,
When on extended wing amain
O'er pine-crown'd height the eagle soars,
And over moor and lake, the crane
Still striveth towards its native shores.

WAGNER.   To strange conceits oft I myself must own,
But impulse such as this I ne'er have known:
Nor woods, nor fields, can long our thoughts engage,
Their wings I envy not the feather'd kind;
Far otherwise the pleasures of the mind,
Bear us from book to book, from page to page!
Then winter nights grow cheerful; keen delight
Warms every limb; and ah! when we unroll
Some old and precious parchment, at the sight
All heaven itself descends upon the soul.

FAUST.   Thy heart by one sole impulse is possess'd;
Unconscious of the other still remain!
Two souls, alas! are lodg'd within my breast,
Which struggle there for undivided reign:
One to the world, with obstinate desire,
And closely-cleaving organs, still adheres;
Above the mist, the other doth aspire,
With sacred vehemence, to purer spheres.
Oh, are there spirits in the air,
Who float 'twixt heaven and earth dominion wielding,
Stoop hither from your golden atmosphere,
Lead me to scenes, new life and fuller yielding!

A magic mantle did I but possess,
Abroad to waft me as on viewless wings,
I'd prize it far beyond the costliest dress,
Now would I change it for the robe of kings.

WAGNER.   Call not the spirits who on mischief wait!
Their troop familiar, streaming through the air,
From every quarter threaten man's estate,
And danger in a thousand forms prepare!
They drive impetuous from the frozen north,
With fangs sharp-piercing, and keen arrowy tongues;
From the ungenial east they issue forth,
And prey, with parching breath, upon thy lungs;
If, waft'd on the desert's flaming wing,
They from the south heap fire upon the brain,
Refreshment from the west at first they bring,
Anon to drown thyself and field and plain.
In wait for mischief, they are prompt to hear;
With guileful purpose our behests obey;
Like ministers of grace they oft appear,
And lisp like angels, to betray.
But let us hence! Grey eve doth all things blend,
The air grows chill, the mists descend!
'Tis in the evening first our home we prize —
Why stand you thus, and gaze with wondering eyes?
What in the gloom thus moves you?

FAUST.   Yon black hound
See'st thou, through corn and stubble scampering round?

WAGNER.   I've mark'd him long, naught strange in him I see!

FAUST.   Note him! What takest thou the brute to be?

WAGNER.   But for a poodle, whom his instinct serves
His master's track to find once more.

FAUST.   Dost mark how round us, with wide spiral curves,
He wheels, each circle closer than before?
And, if I err not, he appears to me
A line of fire upon his track to leave.

WAGNER.   Naught but a poodle black of hue I see;
'Tis some illusion doth your sight deceive.

FAUST.   Methinks a magic coil our feet around,
He for a future snare doth lightly spread.

WAGNER.   Around us as in doubt I see him shyly bound,
Since he two strangers seeth in his master's stead.

FAUST.   The circle narrows, he's already near!
WAGNER.   A dog dost see, no spectre have we here;
        He growls, doubts, lays him on his belly, too,
        And wags his tail — as dogs are wont to do.
FAUST.   Come hither, Sirrah! join our company!
WAGNER.   A very poodle, he appears to be!
        Thou standest still, for thee he'll wait;
        Thou speak'st to him, he fawns upon thee straight;
        Aught thou mayst lose, again he'll bring,
        And for thy stick will into water spring.
FAUST.   Thou'rt right indeed; no traces now I see
        Whatever of a spirit's agency.
        'Tis training — nothing more.
WAGNER.   A dog well taught
        E'en by the wisest of us may be sought.
        Ay, to your favour he's entitled too,
        Apt scholar of the students, 'tis his due!

                                        [*They enter the gate of the town.*]

                            SCENE — *Study*

Enter FAUST *with the poodle.*

FAUST.   Now field and meadow I've forsaken;
        O'er them deep night her veil doth draw;
        In us the better soul doth waken,
        With feelings of foreboding awe,
        All lawless promptings, deeds unholy,
        Now slumber, and all wild desires;
        The love of man doth sway us wholly,
        And love to God the soul inspires.

        Peace, poodle, peace! Scamper not thus; obey me!
        Why at the threshold snuffest thou so?
        Behind the stove now quietly lay thee,
        My softest cushion to thee I'll throw.
        As thou, without, didst please and amuse me
        Running and frisking about on the hill,

So tendance[1] now I will not refuse thee;
A welcome guest, if thou'lt be still.

> Ah! when the friendly taper gloweth,
> Once more within our narrow cell,
> Then in the heart itself that knoweth,
> A light the darkness doth dispel.
> Reason her voice resumes; returneth
> Hope's gracious bloom, with promise rife;
> For streams of life the spirit yearneth,
> Ah! for the very fount of life.

Poodle, snarl not! with the tone that arises,
Hallow'd and peaceful, my soul within,
Accords not thy growl, thy bestial din.
We find it not strange, that man despises
What he conceives not;
That he the good and fair misprizes —
Finding them often beyond his ken;
Will the dog snarl at them like men?

But ah! Despite my will, it stands confessed,
Contentment welleth up no longer in my breast.
Yet wherefore must the stream, alas, so soon be dry,
That we once more athirst should lie?
Full oft this sad experience hath been mine;
Nathless[2] the want admits of compensation;
For things above the earth we learn to pine,
Our spirits yearn for revelation,
Which nowhere burns with purer beauty blent,
Than here in the New Testament.
To ope the ancient text an impulse strong
Impels me, and its sacred lore,
With honest purpose to explore,
And render into my loved German tongue.

> [*He opens a volume, and applies himself to it.*]

'Tis writ, "In the beginning was the Word!"
I pause, perplex'd! Who now will help afford?

---

1. *tendance*] short for attendance; watchful care.
2. *Nathless*] Nevertheless.

I cannot the mere Word so highly prize;
I must translate it otherwise,
If by the spirit guided as I read.
"In the beginning was the Sense!" Take heed,
The import of this primal sentence weigh,
Lest thy too hasty pen be led astray!
Is force creative then of Sense the dower?
"In the beginning was the Power!"
Thus should it stand: yet, while the line I trace,
A something warns me, once more to efface.
The spirit aids! from anxious scruples freed,
I write, "In the beginning was the Deed!"

    Am I with thee my room to share,
    Poodle, thy barking now forbear,
    Forbear thy howling!
    Comrade so noisy, ever growling,
    I cannot suffer here to dwell.
    One or the other, mark me well,
    Forthwith must leave the cell.
    I'm loath the guest-right to withhold;
    The door's ajar, the passage clear;
    But what must now mine eyes behold!
    Are nature's laws suspended here?
    Real is it, or a phantom show?
    In length and breadth how doth my poodle grow!
    He lifts himself with threat'ning mien,
    In likeness of a dog no longer seen!
    What spectre have I harbour'd thus!
    Huge as a hippopotamus,
    With fiery eye, terrific tooth!
    Ah! now I know thee, sure enough!
    For such a base, half-hellish brood,
    The key of Solomon is good.
SPIRITS.   [*Without*] Captur'd there within is one!
    Stay without and follow none!
    Like a fox in iron snare,
    Hell's old lynx is quaking there,
        But take heed!
    Hover round, above, below,
        To and fro,

Then from durance is he freed!
Can ye aid him, spirits all,
Leave him not in mortal thrall!
Many a time and oft hath he
Served us, when at liberty.

FAUST.   The monster to confront, at first,
The spell of Four must be rehears'd;

> Salamander shall kindle,
> Writhe nymph of the wave,
> In air sylph shall dwindle,
> And Kobold shall slave.

Who doth ignore
The primal Four,
Nor knows aright
Their use and might,
O'er spirits will he
Ne'er master be!

> Vanish in the fiery glow,
> Salamander!
> Rushingly together flow.
> Undine!
> Shimmer in the meteor's gleam,
> Sylphide!
> Hither bring thine homely aid,
> Incubus! Incubus!
> Step forth! I do adjure thee thus!

None of the Four
Lurks in the beast:
He grins at me, untroubled as before;
I have not hurt him in the least.
A spell of fear
Thou now shalt hear.

> Art thou, comrade fell,
> Fugitive from Hell?
> See then this sign,
> Before which incline
> The murky troops of Hell!

With bristling hair now doth the creature swell.

> Canst thou, reprobate,
> Read the uncreate,

Unspeakable, diffused
Throughout the heavenly sphere,
Shamefully abused,
Transpierced with nail and spear!

Behind the stove, tam'd by my spells,
Like an elephant he swells;
Wholly now he fills the room,
He into mist will melt away.
Ascend not to the ceiling! Come,
Thyself at the master's feet now lay!
Thou seest that mine is no idle threat.
With holy fire I will scorch thee yet!
Wait not the might
That lies in the triple-glowing light!
Wait not the might
Of all my arts in fullest measure!

[As the mist sinks, MEPHISTOPHELES comes forward from behind the
                     stove, in the dress of a traveling scholar.]

MEPH.   Why all this uproar? What's the master's pleasure?
FAUST.   This then the kernel of the brute!
         A traveling scholar? Why I needs must smile.
MEPH.   Your learned reverence humbly I salute!
         You've made me swelter in a pretty style.
FAUST.   Thy name?
MEPH.   The question trifling seems from one,
         Who it appears the Word doth rate so low;
         Who, undeluded by mere outward show,
         To Being's depths would penetrate alone.
FAUST.   With gentlemen like you indeed
         The inward essence from the name we read,
         As all too plainly it doth appear,
         When Beelzebub, Destroyer, Liar, meets the ear.
         Who then art thou?
MEPH.   Part of that power which still
         Produceth good, whilst ever scheming ill.
FAUST.   What hidden mystery in this riddle lies?
MEPH.   The spirit I, which evermore denies!
         And justly; for whate'er to light is brought
         Deserves again to be reduced to naught;

Then better 'twere that naught should be.
Thus all the elements which ye
Destruction, Sin, or briefly, Evil, name,
As my peculiar element I claim.

FAUST.   Thou nam'st thyself a part, and yet a whole I see.

MEPH.   The modest truth I speak to thee.
Though folly's microcosm, man, it seems,
Himself to be a perfect whole esteems:
Part of the part am I, which at the first was all,
A part of darkness, which gave birth to light,
Proud light, who now his mother would enthrall,
Contesting space and ancient rank with night.
Yet he succeedeth not, for struggle as he will,
To forms material he adhereth still;
From them he streameth, them he maketh fair,
And still the progress of his beams they check;
And so, I trust, when comes the final wreck,
Light will, ere long, the doom of matter share.

FAUST.   Thy worthy avocation now I guess!
Wholesale annihilation won't prevail,
So thou'rt beginning on a smaller scale.

MEPH.   And, to say truth, as yet with small success.
Oppos'd to naught, this clumsy world,
The something — it subsisteth still;
Not yet is it to ruin hurl'd,
Despite the efforts of my will.
Tempests and earthquakes, fire and flood, I've tried;
Yet land and ocean still unchang'd abide!
And then of humankind and beasts, the accursed brood, —
Neither o'er them can I extend my sway.
What countless myriads have I swept away!
Yet ever circulates the fresh young blood.
It is enough to drive me to despair!
As in the earth, in water, and in air,
A thousand germs burst forth spontaneously;
In moisture, drought, heat, cold, they still appear!
Had I not flame selected as my sphere
Nothing apart had been reserved for me.

FAUST.   So thou with thy cold devil's fist
Still clench'd in malice impotent

Dost the creative power resist,
The active, the beneficent!
Henceforth some other task essay,
Of Chaos thou the wondrous son!

MEPH.   We will consider what you say,
And talk about it more anon!
For this time have I leave to go?

FAUST.   Why thou shouldst ask, I cannot see.
Since thee I now have learned to know,
At thy good pleasure, visit me.
Here is the window, here the door,
The chimney, too, may serve thy need.

MEPH.   I must confess, my stepping o'er
Thy threshold a slight hindrance doth impede;
The wizard-foot doth me retain.

FAUST.   The pentagram thy peace doth mar?
To me, thou son of hell, explain,
How camest thou in, if this thine exit bar?
Could such a spirit aught ensnare?

MEPH.   Observe it well, it is not drawn with care,
One of the angles, that which points without,
Is, as thou seest, not quite closed.

FAUST.   Chance hath the matter happily dispos'd!
So thou my captive art? No doubt!
By accident thou thus art caught!

MEPH.   In sprang the dog, indeed, observing naught;
Things now assume another shape,
The devil's in the house and can't escape.

FAUST.   Why through the window not withdraw?

MEPH.   For ghosts and for the devil 'tis a law.
Where they stole in, there they must forth. We're free
The first to choose; as to the second, slaves are we.

FAUST.   E'en hell hath its peculiar laws, I see!
I'm glad of that! a pact may then be made,
The which you gentlemen will surely keep?

MEPH.   What e'er therein is promised thou shalt reap,
No tittle shall remain unpaid.
But such arrangements time require;
We'll speak of them when next we meet;
Most earnestly I now entreat,

This once permission to retire.

FAUST.   Another moment prithee here remain,
Me with some happy word to pleasure.

MEPH.   Now let me go! ere long I'll come again,
Then thou may'st question at thy leisure.

FAUST.   'Twas not my purpose thee to lime;[3]
The snare hast entered of thine own free will:
Let him who holds the devil, hold him still!
So soon he'll catch him not a second time.

MEPH.   If it so please thee, I'm at thy command;
Only on this condition, understand;
That worthily thy leisure to beguile,
I here may exercise my arts awhile.

FAUST.   Thou'rt free to do so! Gladly I'll attend;
But be thine art a pleasant one!

MEPH.   My friend,
This hour enjoyment more intense,
Shall captivate each ravish'd sense,
Than thou could'st compass in the bound
Of the whole year's unvarying round;
And what the dainty spirits sing,
The lovely images they bring,
Are no fantastic sorcery.
Rich odours shall regale your smell,
On choicest sweets your palate dwell,
Your feelings thrill with ecstasy.
No preparation do we need,
Here we together are. Proceed.

SPIRITS.   Hence overshadowing gloom,
Vanish from sight!
O'er us thine azure dome,
Bend, beauteous light!
Dark clouds that o'er us spread,
Melt in thin air!
Stars, your soft radiance shed,
Tender and fair,
Girt with celestial might,
Winging their airy flight,
Spirits are thronging.

3. *to lime*] to entangle.

Follows their forms of light
Infinite longing!
Flutter their vestures bright
O'er field and grove!
Where in their leafy bower
Lovers the livelong hour
Vow deathless love.
Soft bloometh bud and bower!
Bloometh the grove!
Grapes from the spreading vine
Crown the full measure;
Fountains of foaming wine
Gush from the pressure.
Still where the currents wind,
Gems brightly gleam.
Leaving the hills behind
On rolls the stream;
Now into ample seas,
Spreadeth the flood;
Laving the sunny leas,
Mantled with wood.
Rapture the feather'd throng,
Gaily careering,
Sip as they float along;
Sunward they're steering;
On towards the isles of light
Winging their way,
That on the waters bright
Dancingly play.
Hark to the choral strain,
Joyfully ringing!
While on the grassy plain
Dancers are springing;
Climbing the steep hill's side,
Skimming the glassy tide,
Wander they there;
Others on pinions wide
Wing the blue air;
All lifeward tending, upward still wending,
Towards yonder stars that gleam,
Far, far above;

    Stars from whose tender beam
    Rains blissful love.

MEPH. Well done, my dainty spirits! now he slumbers!
  Ye have entranc'd him fairly with your numbers!
  This minstrelsy of yours I must repay, —
  Thou art not yet the man to hold the devil fast! —
  With fairest shapes your spells around him cast,
  And plunge him in a sea of dreams!
  But that this charm be rent, the threshold passed,
  Tooth of rat the way must clear.
  I need not conjure long it seems,
  One rustles hitherward, and soon my voice will hear.
  The master of the rats and mice,
  Of flies and frogs, of bugs and lice,
  Commands thy presence; without fear
  Come forth and gnaw the threshold here,
  Where he with oil has smear'd it. — Thou
  Com'st hopping forth already! Now
  To work! The point that holds me bound
  Is in the outer angle found.
  Another bite — so — now 'tis done —
  Now, Faustus, till we meet again, dream on.

FAUST. [*Awaking*] Am I once more deluded? must I deem
  That thus the throng of spirits disappear?
  The devil's presence, was it but a dream?
  Hath but a poodle scap'd and left me here?

SCENE — *Study*

FAUST, MEPHISTOPHELES.

FAUST. A knock? Come in! Who now would break my rest?
MEPH. 'Tis I!
FAUST.   Come in!
MEPH.   Thrice be the words express'd.
FAUST. Then I repeat, Come in!
MEPH.   'Tis well,
  I hope that we shall soon agree!
  For now your fancies to expel,

Here, as a youth of high degree,
I come in gold-lac'd scarlet vest,
And stiff-silk mantle richly dress'd,
A cock's gay feather for a plume,
A long and pointed rapier, too;
And briefly I would counsel you
To don at once the same costume,
And, free from trammels, speed away,
That what life is you may essay.

FAUST.   In every garb I needs must feel oppress'd,
My heart to earth's low cares a prey.
Too old the trifler's part to play,
Too young to live by no desire possess'd.
What can the world to me afford?
Renounce! renounce! is still the word;
This is the everlasting song
In every ear that ceaseless rings,
And which, alas, our whole life long,
Hoarsely each passing moment sings.
But to new horror I awake each morn,
And I could weep hot tears, to see the sun
Dawn on another day, whose round forlorn
Accomplishes no wish of mine — not one.
Which still, with froward captiousness, impairs
E'en the presentiment of every joy,
While low realities and paltry cares
The spirit's fond imaginings destroy.
Then must I too, when falls the veil of night,
Stretch'd on my pallet languish in despair,
Appalling dreams my soul affright;
No rest vouchsafed me even there.
The god, who throned within my breast resides,
Deep in my soul can stir the springs;
With sovereign sway my energies he guides,
He cannot move external things;
And so existence is to me a weight.
Death fondly I desire, and life I hate.

MEPH.   And yet, methinks, by most 'twill be confess'd
That Death is never quite a welcome guest.

FAUST.   Happy the man around whose brow he binds
The bloodstain'd wreath in conquest's dazzling hour;

Or whom, excited by the dance, he finds
Dissolv'd in bliss, in love's delicious bower!
O that before the lofty spirit's might,
Enraptured, I had rendered up my soul!
MEPH.   Yet did a certain man refrain one night,
Of its brown juice to drain the crystal bowl.
FAUST.   To play the spy diverts you then?
MEPH.   I own,
Though not omniscient, much to me is known.
FAUST.   If o'er my soul the tone familiar, stealing,
Drew me from harrowing thought's bewild'ring maze,
Touching the ling'ring chords of childlike feeling,
With sweet harmonies of happier days:
So curse I all, around the soul that windeth
Its magic and alluring spell,
And with delusive flattery bindeth
Its victim to this dreary cell!
Curs'd before all things be the high opinion,
Wherewith the spirit girds itself around!
Of shows delusive curs'd be the dominion,
Within whose mocking sphere our sense is bound!
Accurs'd of dreams the treacherous wiles,
The cheat of glory, deathless fame!
Accurs'd what each as property beguiles,
Wife, child, slave, plough, whate'er its name!
Accurs'd be mammon, when with treasure
He doth to daring deeds incite:
Or when to steep the soul in pleasure,
He spreads the couch of soft delight!
Curs'd be the grape's balsamic juice!
Accurs'd love's dream, of joys the first!
Accurs'd be hope! accurs'd be faith!
And more than all, be patience curs'd!

CHORUS OF SPIRITS [*Invisible*]

Woe! woe!
Thou hast destroy'd
The beautiful world
With violent blow;
'Tis shiver'd! 'tis shatter'd!

> The fragments abroad by a demigod scatter'd!
> Now we sweep
> The wrecks into nothingness!
> Fondly we weep
> The beauty that's gone!
> Thou, 'mongst the sons of earth,
> Lofty and mighty one,
> Build it once more!
> In thine own bosom the lost world restore!
> Now with unclouded sense
> Enter a new career;
> Songs shall salute thine ear,
> Ne'er heard before!

MEPH.   My little ones these spirits be.
Hark! with shrewd intelligence,
How they recommend to thee
Action, and the joys of sense!
In the busy world to dwell,
Fain they would allure thee hence:
For within this lonely cell,
Stagnate sap of life and sense.

Forbear to trifle longer with thy grief,
Which, vulture-like, consumes thee in this den.
The worst society is some relief,
Making thee feel thyself a man with men.
Nathless, it is not meant, I trow,[1]
To thrust thee 'mid the vulgar throng.
I to the upper ranks do not belong;
Yet if, by me companion'd, thou
Thy steps through life forthwith wilt take,
Upon the spot myself I'll make
Thy comrade; —
Should it suit thy need,
I am thy servant, am thy slave indeed!
FAUST.   And how must I thy services repay?
MEPH.   Thereto thou lengthen'd respite hast!
FAUST.   No! No!

---

1. *trow*] believe, think.

      The devil is an egoist I know:
      And, for Heaven's sake, 'tis not his way
      Kindness to any one to show.
      Let the condition plainly be exprest!
      Such a domestic is a dangerous guest.

MEPH.   I'll pledge myself to be thy servant *here*,
      Still at thy back alert and prompt to be;
      But when together *yonder* we appear,
      Then shalt thou do the same for me.

FAUST.   But small concern I feel for yonder world;
      Hast thou this system into ruin hurl'd,
      Another may arise the void to fill.
      This earth the fountain whence my pleasures flow,
      This sun doth daily shine upon my woe,
      And if this world I must forego,
      Let happen then, — what can and will.
      I to this theme will close mine ears,
      If men hereafter hate and love,
      And if there be in yonder spheres
      A depth below or height above.

MEPH.   In this mood thou mayst venture it. But make
      The compact! I at once will undertake
      To charm thee with mine arts. I'll give thee more
      Than mortal eye hath e'er beheld before.

FAUST.   What, sorry Devil, hast thou to bestow?
      Was ever mortal spirit, in its high endeavour,
      Fathom'd by Being such as thou?
      Yet food thou hast which satisfieth never,
      Hast ruddy gold, that still doth flow
      Like restless quicksilver away,
      A game thou hast, at which none win who play,
      A girl who would, with amorous eyen,
      E'en from my breast, a neighbour snare,
      Lofty ambition's joy divine,
      That, meteor-like, dissolves in air.
      Show me the fruit that, ere 'tis pluck'd, doth rot,
      And trees, whose verdure daily buds anew!

MEPH.   Such a commission scares me not,
      I can provide such treasures, it is true;
      But, my good friend, a season will come round,
      When on what's good we may regale in peace.

FAUST.   If e'er upon my couch, stretched at my ease, I'm found,
    Then may my life that instant cease!
    Me canst thou cheat with glozing[2] wile
    Till self-reproach away I cast, —
    Me with joy's lure canst thou beguile; —
    Let that day be for me the last!
    Be this our wager!

MEPH.   Settled!
FAUST.   Sure and fast!
    When to the moment I shall say,
    "Linger awhile! so fair thou art!"
    Then mayst thou fetter me straightway,
    Then to the abyss will I depart!
    Then may the solemn death-bell sound,
    Then from thy service thou art free,
    The index then may cease its round.
    And time be never more for me!
MEPH.   I shall remember: pause, ere 'tis too late.
FAUST.   Thereto a perfect right hast thou.
    My strength I do not rashly overrate.
    Slave am I here, at any rate,
    If thine, or whose, it matters not, I trow.
MEPH.   At thine inaugural feast I will this day
    Attend, my duties to commence. —
    But one thing! — Accidents may happen, hence
    A line or two in writing grant, I pray.
FAUST.   A writing, Pedant! dost demand from me?
    Man, and man's plighted word, are these unknown to thee?
    Is't not enough, that by the word I gave,
    My doom for evermore is cast?
    Doth not the world in all its currents rave,
    And must a promise hold me fast?
    Yet fixed is this delusion in our heart;
    Who, of his own free will, therefrom would part?
    How blest within whose breast truth reigneth pure!
    No sacrifice will he repent when made!
    A formal deed, with seal and signature,
    A spectre this from which all shrink afraid.
    The word its life resigneth in the pen,

---

2. *glozing*] deceptively flattering.

Leather and wax usurp the mastery then.
Spirit of evil! what dost thou require?
Brass, marble, parchment, paper, dost desire?
Shall I with chisel, pen, or graver write?
Thy choice is free; to me 'tis all the same.

MEPH. Wherefore thy passion so excite
And thus thine eloquence inflame?
A scrap is for our compact good.
Thou under-signest merely with a drop of blood.

FAUST. If this will satisfy thy mind,
Thy whim I'll gratify, howe'er absurd.

MEPH. Blood is a juice of very special kind.

FAUST. Be not afraid that I shall break my word!
The scope of all my energy
Is in exact accordance with my vow.
Vainly I have aspired too high;
I'm on a level but with such as thou;
Me the great spirit scorn'd, defied;
Nature from me herself doth hide;
Rent is the web of thought; my mind
Doth knowledge loathe of every kind.
In depths of sensual pleasure drown'd,
Let us our fiery passions still!
Enwrapp'd in magic's veil profound,
Let wondrous charms our senses thrill!
Plunge we in time's tempestuous flow,
Stem we the rolling surge of chance!
There may alternate weal and woe,
Success and failure, as they can,
Mingle and shift in changeful dance!
Excitement is the sphere for man.

MEPH. Nor goal, nor measure is prescrib'd to you,
If you desire to taste of every thing,
To snatch at joy while on the wing,
May your career amuse and profit too!
Only fall to and don't be over coy!

FAUST. Hearken! The end I aim at is not joy;
I crave excitement, agonizing bliss,
Enamour'd hatred, quickening vexation.
Purg'd from the love of knowledge, my vocation,
The scope of all my powers henceforth be this,

To bare my breast to every pang, — to know
In my heart's core all human weal and woe,
To grasp in thought the lofty and the deep,
Men's various fortunes on my breast to heap,
And thus to theirs dilate my individual mind,
And share at length with them the shipwreck of mankind.

MEPH.   Oh, credit me, who still as ages roll,
Have chew'd this bitter fare from year to year,
No mortal, from the cradle to the bier,
Digests the ancient leaven! Know, this Whole
Doth for the Deity alone subsist!
He in eternal brightness doth exist,
Us unto darkness he hath brought, and here
Where day and night alternate, is your sphere.

FAUST.   But 'tis my will!

MEPH.   Well spoken, I admit!
But one thing puzzles me, my friend;
Time's short, art long; methinks 'twere fit
That you to friendly counsel should attend.
A poet choose as your ally!
Let him thought's wide dominion sweep,
Each good and noble quality,
Upon your honoured brow to heap;
The lion's magnanimity,
The fleetness of the hind,
The fiery blood of Italy,
The Northern's steadfast mind.
Let him to you the mystery show
To blend high aims and cunning low;
And while youth's passions are aflame
To fall in love by rule and plan!
I fain would meet with such a man;
Would him Sir Microcosmus name.

FAUST.   What then am I, if I aspire in vain
The crown of our humanity to gain,
Towards which my every sense doth strain?

MEPH.   Thou'rt after all — just what thou art.
Put on thy head a wig with countless locks,
And to a cubit's height upraise thy socks,
Still thou remainest ever, what thou art.

FAUST.   I feel it, I have heap'd upon my brain

The gather'd treasure of man's thought in vain;
And when at length from studious toil I rest,
No power, new-born, springs up within my breast;
A hair's breadth is not added to my height,
I am no nearer to the infinite.

MEPH.   Good sir, these things you view indeed,
Just as by other men they're view'd;
We must more cleverly proceed,
Before life's joys our grasp elude.
The devil! thou hast hands and feet,
And head and heart are also thine;
What I enjoy with relish sweet,
Is it on that account less mine?
If for six stallions I can pay,
Do I not own their strength and speed?
A proper man I dash away,
As their two dozen legs were mine indeed.
Up then, from idle pondering free,
And forth into the world with me!
I tell you what; — your speculative churl
Is like a beast which some ill spirit leads,
On barren wilderness, in ceaseless whirl,
While all around lie fair and verdant meads.

FAUST.   But how shall we begin?

MEPH.   We will go hence with speed,
A place of torment this indeed!
A precious life, thyself to bore,
And some few youngsters evermore!
Leave that to neighbour Paunch! — withdraw,
Why wilt thou plague thyself with thrashing straw?
The very best that thou dost know
Thou dar'st not to the striplings show.
One in the passage now doth wait!

FAUST.   I'm in no mood to see him now.

MEPH.   Poor lad! He must be tired, I trow;
He must not go disconsolate.
Hand me thy cap and gown; the mask
Is for my purpose quite first rate.   [*He changes his dress.*]

Now leave it to my wit! I ask
But quarter of an hour; meanwhile equip,
And make all ready for our pleasant trip!   [*Exit* FAUST.]

MEPH.   [*In* FAUST'*s long gown*] Mortal! the loftiest attributes of men,
Reason and Knowledge, only thus contemn,
Still let the Prince of lies, without control,
With shows, and mocking charms delude thy soul,
I have thee unconditionally then!
Fate hath endow'd him with an ardent mind,
Which unrestrain'd still presses on for ever,
And whose precipitate endeavour
Earth's joys o'erleaping, leaveth them behind.
Him will I drag through life's wild waste,
Through scenes of vapid dulness, where at last
Bewilder'd, he shall falter, and stick fast;
And, still to mock his greedy haste,
Viands and drink shall float his craving lips beyond —
Vainly he'll seek refreshment, anguish-tost,
And were he not the devil's by his bond,
Yet must his soul infallibly be lost!

A STUDENT *enters*

STUDENT.   But recently I've quitted home,
Full of devotion am I come
A man to know and hear, whose name
With reverence is known to fame.

MEPH.   Your courtesy much flatters me!
A man like other men you see;
Pray have you yet applied elsewhere?

STUDENT.   I would entreat your friendly care!
I've youthful blood and courage high;
Of gold I bring a fair supply;
To let me go my mother was not fain;
But here I longed true knowledge to attain.

MEPH.   You've hit upon the very place.

STUDENT.   And yet my steps I would retrace.
These walls, this melancholy room,
O'erpower me with a sense of gloom;

The space is narrow, nothing green,
No friendly tree is to be seen:
And in these halls, with benches filled, distraught,
Sight, hearing fail me, and the power of thought.

MEPH.   It all depends on habit. Thus at first
The infant takes not kindly to the breast,
But before long, its eager thirst
Is fain to slake with hearty zest:
Thus at the breasts of wisdom day by day
With keener relish you'll your thirst allay.

STUDENT.   Upon her neck I fain would hang with joy;
To reach it, say, what means must I employ?

MEPH.   Explain, ere further time we lose,
What special faculty you choose?

STUDENT.   Profoundly learned I would grow,
What heaven contains would comprehend,
O'er earth's wide realm my gaze extend,
Nature and science I desire to know.

MEPH.   You are upon the proper track, I find;
Take heed, let nothing dissipate your mind.

STUDENT.   My heart and soul are in the chase!
Though to be sure I fain would seize,
On pleasant summer holidays,
A little liberty and careless ease.

MEPH.   Use well your time, so rapidly it flies;
Method will teach you time to win;
Hence, my young friend, I would advise,
With college logic to begin!
Then will your mind be so well braced,
In Spanish boots so tightly laced,
That on 'twill circumspectly creep,
Thought's beaten track securely keep,
Nor will it, ignis-fatuus like,
Into the path of error strike.
Then many a day they'll teach you how
The mind's spontaneous acts, till now
As eating and as drinking free,
Require a process; — one! two! three!
In truth the subtle web of thought
Is like the weaver's fabric wrought:
One treadle moves a thousand lines,

Swift dart the shuttles to and fro,
Unseen the threads together flow,
A thousand knots one stroke combines.
Then forward steps your sage to show,
And prove to you, it must be so;
The first being so, and so the second,
The third and fourth deduc'd we see;
And if there were no first and second,
Nor third nor fourth would ever be.
This, scholars of all countries prize, —
Yet 'mong themselves no weavers rise. —
He who would know and treat of aught alive,
Seeks first the living spirit thence to drive:
Then are the lifeless fragments in his hand,
There only fails, alas! the spirit-band.
This process, chemists name, in learned thesis,
Mocking themselves, *Naturæ encheiresis*.[3]

STUDENT.   Your words I cannot fully comprehend.

MEPH.   In a short time you will improve, my friend,
When of scholastic forms you learn the use;
And how by method all things to reduce.

STUDENT.   So doth all this my brain confound,
As if a mill-wheel there were turning round.

MEPH.   And next, before aught else you learn,
You must with zeal to metaphysics turn!
There see that you profoundly comprehend,
What doth the limit of man's brain transcend;
For that which is or is not in the head
A sounding phrase will serve you in good stead.
But before all strive this half year
From one fix'd order ne'er to swerve!
Five lectures daily you must hear;
The hour still punctually observe!
Yourself with studious zeal prepare,
And closely in your manual look,
Hereby may you be quite aware
That all he utters standeth in the book;
Yet write away without cessation,
As at the Holy Ghost's dictation!

3. *Naturæ encheiresis*] an operation on nature.

STUDENT.   This, Sir, a second time you need not say!
    Your counsel I appreciate quite;
    What we possess in black and white,
    We can in peace and comfort bear away.
MEPH.   A faculty I pray you name.
STUDENT.   For jurisprudence, some distaste I own.
MEPH.   To me this branch of science is well known,
    And hence I cannot your repugnance blame.
    Customs and laws in every place,
-    Like a disease, an heir-loom dread,
    Still trail their curse from race to race,
    And furtively abroad they spread.
    To nonsense, reason's self they turn;
    Beneficence becomes a pest;
    Woe unto thee, that thou'rt a grandson born!
    As for the law born with us, unexpressed; —
    That law, alas, none careth to discern.
STUDENT.   You deepen my dislike. The youth
    Whom you instruct, is blest in sooth!
    To try theology I feel inclined.
MEPH.   I would not lead you willingly astray,
    But as regards this science, you will find
    So hard it is to shun the erring way,
    And so much hidden poison lies therein,
    Which scarce can you discern from medicine.
    Here too it is the best, to listen but to one,
    And by the master's words to swear alone.
    To sum up all — To words hold fast!
    Then the safe gate securely pass'd,
    You'll reach the fane[4] of certainty at last.
STUDENT.   But then some meaning must the words convey.
MEPH.   Right! But o'er-anxious thought, you'll find of no avail,
    For there precisely where ideas fail,
    A word comes opportunely into play;
    Most admirable weapons words are found,
    On words a system we securely ground,
    In words we can conveniently believe,
    Nor of a single jot can we a word bereave.

    4. *fane*] church, temple.

STUDENT. Your pardon for my importunity;
  Yet once more must I trouble you:
  On medicine, I'll thank you to supply
  A pregnant utterance or two!
  Three years! how brief the appointed tide!
  The field, heaven knows, is all too wide!
  If but a friendly hint be thrown,
  'Tis easier then to feel one's way.
MEPH. [Aside] I'm weary of the dry pedantic tone,
  And must again the genuine devil play.
  [Aloud] Of medicine the spirit's caught with ease,
  The great and little world you study through,
  That things may then their course pursue,
  As heaven may please.
  In vain abroad you range through science's ample space,
  Each man learns only that which learn he can;
  Who knows the moment to embrace,
  He is your proper man.
  In person you are tolerably made,
  Nor in assurance will you be deficient:
  Self-confidence acquire, be not afraid,
  Others will then esteem you a proficient.
  Learn chiefly with the sex to deal!
  Their thousand ahs and ohs,
  These the sage doctor knows,
  He only from one point can heal.
  Assume a decent tone of courteous ease,
  You have them then to humour as you please.
  First a diploma must belief infuse,
  That you in your profession take the lead:
  You then at once those easy freedoms use
  For which another many a year must plead;
  Learn how to feel with nice address
  The dainty wrist; — and how to press,
  With ardent furtive glance, the slender waist,
  To feel how tightly it is laced.
STUDENT. There is some sense in that! one sees the how and why.
MEPH. Grey is, young friend, all theory:
  And green of life the golden tree.

STUDENT.   I swear it seemeth like a dream to me.
    May I some future time repeat my visit,
    To hear on what your wisdom grounds your views?
MEPH.   Command my humble service when you choose.
STUDENT.   Ere I retire, one boon I must solicit:
    Here is my album, do not, Sir, deny
    This token of your favour!
MEPH.   ·   Willingly!

> [*He writes and returns the book.*]

STUDENT. [*Reads*] ERITIS SICUT DEUS, SCIENTES BONUM ET
    MALUM[5]

> [*He reverently closes the book and retires.*]

MEPH.   Let but this ancient proverb be your rule,
    My cousin follow still, the wily snake,
    And with your likeness to the gods, poor fool,
    Ere long be sure your poor sick heart will quake!

Enter FAUST.

FAUST.   Whither away?
MEPH.   'Tis thine our course to steer.
    The little world, and then the great we'll view.
    With what delight, what profit too,
    Thou'lt revel through thy gay career!
FAUST.   Despite my length of beard I need
    The easy manners that insure success;
    Th' attempt I fear can ne'er succeed;
    To mingle in the world I want address;
    I still have an embarrass'd air, and then
    I feel myself so small with other men.
MEPH.   Time, my good friend, will all that's needful give;
    Be only self-possessed, and thou hast learn'd to live.
FAUST.   But how are we to start, I pray?
    Steeds, servants, carriage, where are they?
MEPH.   We've but to spread this mantle wide,
    'Twill serve whereon through air to ride,
    No heavy baggage need you take,

5. *Eritis . . . malum*] You shall be like God, knowing good and bad.

When we our bold excursion make,
A little gas, which I will soon prepare,
Lifts us from earth; aloft through air,
Light laden, we shall swiftly steer; —
I wish you joy of your new life-career.

SCENE — *Auerbach's Cellar in Leipzig* — A Drinking Party

FROSCH, BRANDER, SIEBEL, ALTMAYER *and* CHORUS.

FROSCH.   No drinking? Naught a laugh to raise?
    None of your gloomy looks, I pray!
    You, who so bright were wont to blaze,
    Are dull as wetted straw to-day.
BRANDER.   'Tis all your fault; your part you do not bear,
    No beastliness, no folly.
FROSCH.   [*Pours a glass of wine over his head*] There,
    You have them both!
BRANDER.   You double beast !
FROSCH.   'Tis what you ask'd me for, at least!
SIEBEL.   Whoever quarrels, turn him out!
    With open throat drink, roar, and shout.
    Hollo! Hollo! Ho!
ALT.   Zounds, fellow, cease your deaf'ning cheers!
    Bring cotton-wool! He splits my ears.
SIEBEL.   'Tis when the roof rings back the tone,
    Then first the full power of the bass is known.
FROSCH.   Right! out with him who takes offence!
    A! tara lara da!
ALT.   A! tara lara da!
FROSCH.   Our throats are tuned. Come let's commence!

[*Sings*]

    The holy Roman empire now,
    How holds it still together?

BRANDER.   An ugly song! a song political!
    A song offensive! Thank God, every morn
    To rule the Roman empire, that you were not born!

I bless my stars at least that mine is not
Either a kaiser's or a chancellor's lot.
Yet 'mong ourselves should one still lord it o'er the rest;
That we elect a pope I now suggest.
Ye know, what quality ensures
A man's success, his rise secures.

FROSCH.   [*Sings*]

> Bear, lady nightingale above,
> Ten thousand greetings to my love.

SIEBEL.   No greetings to a sweetheart! No love-songs shall there be!
FROSCH.   Love-greetings and love kisses! Thou shalt not hinder me!

[*Sings*]

> Undo the bolt! in silly night,
> Undo the bolt! the lover wakes.
> Shut to the bolt! when morning breaks.

SIEBEL.   Ay, sing, sing on, praise her with all thy might!
My turn to laugh will come some day.
Me hath she jilted once, you the same trick she'll play.
Some gnome her lover be! where cross-roads meet,
With her to play the fool; or old he-goat,
From Blocksberg coming in swift gallop, bleat
A good night to her, from his hairy throat!
A proper lad of genuine flesh and blood,
Is for the damsel far too good;
The greeting she shall have from me,
To smash her window-panes will be!
BRANDER.   [*Striking on the table*] Silence! Attend! to me give ear!
Confess, sirs, I know how to live:
Some love-sick folk are sitting here!
Hence, 'tis but fit, their hearts to cheer,
That I a good-night strain to them should give.
Hark! of the newest fashion is my song!
Strike boldly in the chorus, clear and strong!

[*Sings*]

> Once in a cellar lived a rat,
> He feasted there on butter,
> Until his paunch became as fat
> As that of Doctor Luther.

    The cook laid poison for the guest,
    Then was his heart with pangs oppress'd,
    As if his frame love wasted.

CHORUS [*Shouting*]

As if his frame love wasted.

BRANDER.   He ran around, he ran abroad,
    Of every puddle drinking.
    The house with rage he scratch'd and gnaw'd,
    In vain, — he fast was sinking;
    Full many an anguish'd bound he gave,
    Nothing the hapless brute could save,
    As if his frame love wasted.

CHORUS

As if his frame love wasted.

BRANDER.   By torture driven, in open day,
    The kitchen he invaded,
    Convulsed upon the hearth he lay,
    With anguish sorely jaded;
    The poisoner laugh'd, Ha! ha! quoth she,
    His life is ebbing fast, I see,
    As if his frame love wasted.

CHORUS

As if his frame love wasted.

SIEBEL.   How the dull boors exulting shout!
    Poison for the poor rats to strew
    A fine exploit it is no doubt.
BRANDER.   They, as it seems, stand well with you!
ALT.   Old bald-pate! with the paunch profound!
    The rat's mishap hath tamed his nature;
    For he his counterpart hath found
    Depicted in the swollen creature.

FAUST, MEPHISTOPHELES.

MEPH.   I now must introduce to you
    Before aught else, this jovial crew,
    To show how lightly life may glide away;
    With the folk here each day's a holiday.
    With little wit and much content,

Each on his own small round intent,
Like sportive kitten with its tail;
While no sick-headache they bewail,
And while their host will credit give,
Joyous and free from care they live.
BRANDER.　They're off a journey, that is clear,—
From their strange manners; they have scarce been here
An hour.
FROSCH.　　You're right! Leipzig's the place for me!
'Tis quite a little Paris; people there
Acquire a certain easy finish'd air.
SIEBEL.　What take you now these travellers to be?
FROSCH.　Let me alone! O'er a full glass you'll see,
As easily I'll worm their secret out,
As draw an infant's tooth. I've not a doubt
That my two gentlemen are nobly born,
They look dissatisfied and full of scorn.
BRANDER.　They are but mountebanks, I'll lay a bet!
ALT.　Most like.
FROSCH.　　　　Mark me, I'll screw it from them yet!
MEPH.　[*To* FAUST] These fellows would not scent the devil out,
E'en though he had them by the very throat!
FAUST.　Good-morrow, gentlemen!
SIEBEL.　　　　　　　　　　Thanks for your fair salute.

[*Aside, glancing at* MEPHISTOPHELES.]

How! goes the fellow on a halting foot?
MEPH.　Is it permitted here with you to sit?
Then though good wine is not forthcoming here,
Good company at least our hearts will cheer.
ALT.　A dainty gentleman, no doubt of it.
FROSCH.　You're doubtless recently from Rippach? Pray,
Did you with Master Hans there chance to sup?
MEPH.　To-day we pass'd him, but we did not stop!
When last we met him he had much to say
Touching his cousins, and to each he sent
Full many a greeting and kind compliment.

[*With an inclination towards* FROSCH.]

ALT.　[*Aside to* FROSCH] You have it there!
SIEBEL.　　　　　　　　　　Faith! he's a knowing one!

FROSCH.   Have patience! I will show him up anon!
MEPH.   We heard erewhile, unless I'm wrong,
Voices well trained in chorus pealing?
Certes, most choicely here must song
Re-echo from this vaulted ceiling!
FROSCH.   That you're an amateur one plainly sees!
MEPH.   Oh no, though strong the love, I cannot boast much skill.
ALT.   Give us a song!
MEPH.   As many as you will.
SIEBEL.   But be it a brand new one, if you please!
MEPH.   But recently returned from Spain are we,
The pleasant land of wine and minstrelsy.

> [*Sings*]
>
> A king there was once reigning,
> Who had a goodly flea —

FROSCH.   Hark! did you rightly catch the words? A flea!
An odd sort of a guest he needs must be.
MEPH.   [*Sings*]

> A king there was once reigning,
> Who had a goodly flea,
> Him loved he without feigning,
> As his own son were he!
> His tailor then he summon'd,
> The tailor to him goes:
> Now measure me the youngster
> For jerkin and for hose!

BRANDER.   Take proper heed, the tailor strictly charge,
The nicest measurement to take,
And as he loves his head, to make
The hose quite smooth and not too large!
MEPH.   In satin and in velvet,

> Behold the yonker dressed;
> Bedizen'd o'er with ribbons,
> A cross upon his breast.
> Prime minister they made him,
> He wore a star of state;
> And all his poor relations
> Were courtiers, rich and great.
>
> The gentlemen and ladies

At court were sore distressed;
The queen and all her maidens
Were bitten by the pest,
And yet they dared not scratch them,
Or chase the fleas away.
If we are bit, we catch them,
And crack without delay.

CHORUS [*Shouting*]

If we are bit, &c.

FROSCH.   Bravo! That's the song for me!
SIEBEL.   Such be the fate of every flea!
BRANDER.   With clever finger catch and kill!
ALT.   Hurrah for wine and freedom still!
MEPH.   Were but your wine a trifle better, friend,
  A glass to freedom I would gladly drain.
SIEBEL.   You'd better not repeat those words again!
MEPH.   I am afraid the landlord to offend;
  Else freely I would treat each worthy guest
  From our own cellar to the very best.
SIEBEL.   Out with it then! Your doings I'll defend.
FROSCH.   Give a good glass, and straight we'll praise you, one and all.
  Only let not your samples be too small;
  For if my judgment you desire,
  Certes, an ample mouthful I require.
ALT.   [*Aside*] I guess they're from the Rhenish land.
MEPH.   Fetch me a gimlet here!
BRANDER.   Say, what therewith to bore?
  You cannot have the wine-casks at the door?
ALT.   Our landlord's tool-basket behind doth yonder stand.
MEPH.   [*Takes the gimlet*]
  [*To* FROSCH] Now only say! what liquor will you take?
FROSCH.   How mean you that? have you of every sort?
MEPH.   Each may his own selection make.
ALT.   [*To* FROSCH] Ha! Ha! You lick your lips already at the thought.
FROSCH.   Good, if I have my choice, the Rhenish I propose;
  For still the fairest gifts the fatherland bestows.

[MEPHISTOPHELES *boring a hole in the edge of the
  table opposite to where* FROSCH *is sitting*]

MEPH.   Give me a little wax — and make some stoppers — quick!

ALT.   Why, this is nothing but a juggler's trick!

MEPH.   [*To* BRANDER] And you?

BRANDER.   Champagne's the wine for me;
    Right brisk, and sparkling let it be!

[MEPHISTOPHELES *bores; one of the party has in the meantime prepared*
                  the wax-stoppers and stopped the holes.]

BRANDER.   What foreign is one always can't decline,
    What's good is often scatter'd far apart.
    The French your genuine German hates with all his heart,
    Yet has a relish for their wine.

SIEBEL.   [*As* MEPHISTOPHELES *approaches him*] I like not acid wine, I
    must allow,
    Give me a glass of genuine sweet!

MEPH. [*Bores*]   Tokay
    Shall, if you wish it, flow without delay.

ALT.   Come! look me in the face! no fooling now!
    You are but making fun of us, I trow.

MEPH.   Ah! ah! that would indeed be making free
    With such distinguished guests. Come, no delay;
    What liquor can I serve you with, I pray?

ALT.   Only be quick, it matters not to me.

               [*After the holes are bored and stopped.*]

MEPH.   [*With strange gestures*] Grapes the vine-stock bears,
             Horns the buck-goat wears!
             Wine is sap, the vine is wood,
             The wooden board yields wine as good.
             With a deeper glance and true
             The mysteries of nature view!
             Have faith and here's a miracle!
             Your stoppers draw and drink your fill!

ALL.   [*As they draw the stoppers and the wine chosen by each runs into*
    his glass] Oh beauteous spring, which flows so far!

MEPH.   Spill not a single drop, of this beware!

                    [*They drink repeatedly.*]

ALL.

                [*Sing*]

        Happy as cannibals are we,
        Or as five hundred swine.

MEPH.   They're in their glory, mark their elevation!
FAUST.   Let's hence, nor here our stay prolong.
MEPH.   Attend, of brutishness ere long
        You'll see a glorious revelation.

> [SIEBEL *drinks carelessly; the wine is spilt upon the ground,
> and turns to flame.*]

SIEBEL.   Help! fire! help! Hell is burning!
MEPH.   [*Addressing the flames*]   Stop,
        Kind element, be still, I say!   [*To the Company*]
        Of purgatorial fire as yet 'tis but a drop.
SIEBEL.   What means the knave! For this you'll dearly pay!
        Us, it appears, you do not know.
FROSCH.   Such tricks a second time he'd better show!
ALT.   Methinks 'twere well we pack'd him quietly away.
SIEBEL.   What, sir! with us your hocus-pocus play!
MEPH.   Silence, old wine-cask!
SIEBEL.   How! add insult, too!
        Vile broomstick!
BRANDER.   Hold, or blows shall rain on you!

[ALTMAYER *draws a stopper out of the table; fire springs out against him.*]

ALT.   I burn! I burn!
SIEBEL.   'Tis sorcery, I vow!
        Strike home! The fellow is fair game, I trow!

> [*They draw their knives and attack* MEPHISTOPHELES.]

MEPH.   [*With solemn gestures*]

> Visionary scenes appear!
> Words delusive cheat the ear!
> Be ye there, and be ye here!

> [*They stand amazed and gaze at each other.*]

ALT.   Where am I? What a beauteous land!
FROSCH.   Vineyards! unless my sight deceives?
SIEBEL.   And clust'ring grapes too, close at hand!
BRANDER.   And underneath the spreading leaves,
        What stems there be! What grapes I see!

> [*He seizes* SIEBEL *by the nose. The others reciprocally do the
> same, and raise their knives.*]

MEPH.　[*As above*] Delusion, from their eyes the bandage take!
　　Note how the devil loves a jest to break!

[*He disappears with* FAUST; *the fellows draw back from one another.*]

SIEBEL.　What was it?
ALT.　　　　　　　How?
FROSCH.　　　　　　　　Was that your nose?
BRANDER.　[*To* SIEBEL] And look, my hand doth thine enclose!
ALT.　I felt a shock, it went through every limb!
　　A chair! I'm fainting! All things swim!
FROSCH.　Say what has happened, what's it all about?
SIEBEL.　Where is the fellow? Could I scent him out,
　　His body from his soul I'd soon divide!
ALT.　With my own eyes, upon a cask astride,
　　Forth through the cellar-door I saw him ride —
　　Heavy as lead my feet are growing.　　　[*Turning to the table.*]
　　I wonder is the wine still flowing!
SIEBEL.　'Twas all delusion, cheat and lie.
FROSCH.　'Twas wine I drank, most certainly.
BRANDER.　But with the grapes how was it, pray?
ALT.　That none may miracles believe, who now will say?

SCENE — *Witches' Kitchen*

*A large caldron hangs over the fire on a low hearth; various figures appear
in the vapour rising from it. A* FEMALE MONKEY *sits beside the caldron to
skim it, and watch that it does not boil over. The* MALE MONKEY *with the
young ones is seated near, warming himself. The walls and ceiling are
adorned with the strangest articles of witch-furniture.*

FAUST, MEPHISTOPHELES.

FAUST.　This senseless, juggling witchcraft I detest!
　　Dost promise that in this foul nest
　　Of madness, I shall be restored?
　　Must I seek counsel from an ancient dame?

And can she, by these rites abhorred,
Take thirty winters from my frame?
Woe's me, if thou naught better canst suggest!
Hope has already fled my breast.
Has neither nature nor a noble mind
A balsam yet devis'd of any kind?

MEPH.   My friend, you now speak sensibly. In truth,
Nature a method giveth to renew thy youth:
But in another book the lesson's writ; —
It forms a curious chapter, I admit.

FAUST.   I fain would know it.

MEPH.   Good! A remedy
Without physician, gold, or sorcery:
Away forthwith, and to the fields repair,
Begin to delve, to cultivate the ground,
Thy senses and thyself confine
Within the very narrowest round,
Support thyself upon the simplest fare,
Live like a very brute the brutes among,
Neither esteem it robbery
The acre thou dost reap, thyself to dung;
This is the best method, credit me,
Again at eighty to grow hale and young.

FAUST.   I am not used to it, nor can myself degrade
So far, as in my hand to take the spade.
This narrow life would suit me not at all.

MEPH.   Then we the witch must summon after all.

FAUST.   Will none but this old beldame do?
Canst not thyself the potion brew?

MEPH.   A pretty play our leisure to beguile!
A thousand bridges I could build meanwhile.
Not science only and consummate art,
Patience must also bear her part.
A quiet spirit worketh whole years long;
Time only makes the subtle ferment strong.
And all things that belong thereto,
Are wondrous and exceeding rare!
The devil taught her, it is true;

But yet the draught the devil can't prepare.
[*Perceiving the beasts*] Look yonder, what a dainty pair!
Here is the maid! the knave is there!
[*To the beasts*] It seems your dame is not at home?
THE MONKEYS.   Gone to carouse,
              Out of the house,
              Thro' the chimney and away!
MEPH.   How long is it her wont to roam?
THE MONKEYS.   While we can warm our paws she'll stay.
MEPH.   [*To* FAUST] What think you of the charming creatures?
FAUST.   I loathe alike their form and features!
MEPH.   Nay, such discourse, be it confessed,
  Is just the thing that pleases me the best.
  [*To the* MONKEYS] Tell me, ye whelps, accursed crew!
  What stir ye in the broth about?
THE MONKEYS.   Coarse beggar's gruel here we stew.
MEPH.   Of customers you'll have a rout.
THE HE-MONKEY.   [*Approaching and fawning on* MEPHISTOPHELES]
                  Quick! quick! throw the dice,
                  Make me rich in a trice,
                  Oh give me the prize!
                  Alas, for myself!
                  Had I plenty of pelf,[1]
                  I then should be wise.
MÉPH.   How blest the ape would think himself, if he
  Could only put into the lottery!

[*In the meantime the young* MONKEYS *have been playing with a large
                  globe, which they roll forwards.*]

THE HE-MONKEY.   The world behold;
                  Unceasingly roll'd,
                  It riseth and falleth ever;
                  It ringeth like glass!
                  How brittle, alas!
                  'Tis hollow, and resteth never.

1. *pelf*] money, riches.

How bright the sphere,
Still brighter here!
Now living am I!
Dear son, beware!
Nor venture there!
Thou too must die!
It is of clay;
'Twill crumble away;
There fragments lie.

MEPH.   Of what use is the sieve?
THE HE-MONKEY.   [*Taking it down*] The sieve would show,
          If thou wert a thief or no?

[*He runs to the* SHE-MONKEY, *and makes her look through it.*]

Look through the sieve!
Dost know him the thief,
And dar'st thou not call him so?

MEPH.   [*Approaching the fire*] And then this pot?
THE MONKEYS.   The half-witted sot!
          He knows not the pot!
          He knows not the kettle!
MEPH.   Unmannerly beast!
          Be civil at least!
THE HE-MONKEY.   Take the whisk and sit down on the settle!

[*He makes* MEPHISTOPHELES *sit down.*]

FAUST.   [*Who all this time has been standing before a looking-glass, now
     approaching, and now retiring from it*] What do I see? what form,
        whose charms transcend
  The loveliness of earth, is mirror'd here!
  O Love, to waft me to her sphere,
  To me the swiftest of thy pinions lend!
  Alas! If I remain not rooted to this place,
  If to approach more near I'm fondly lur'd,
  Her image fades, in veiling mist obscur'd! —
  Model of beauty both in form and face!
  Is't possible? Hath woman charms so rare?
  In this recumbent form, supremely fair,
  The essence must I see of heavenly grace?
  Can aught so exquisite on earth be found?

MEPH.   The six days' labour of a god, my friend,
Who doth himself cry bravo, at the end,
By something clever doubtless should be crown'd.
For this time gaze your fill, and when you please
Just such a prize for you I can provide;
How blest is he to whom kind fate decrees,
To take her to his home, a lovely bride!

[FAUST *continues to gaze into the mirror.* MEPHISTOPHELES, *stretching himself on the settle and playing with the whisk, continues to speak.*]

Here sit I, like a king upon his throne;
My sceptre this; — the crown I want alone.

THE MONKEYS. [*Who have hitherto been making all sorts of strange gestures, bring* MEPHISTOPHELES *a crown, with loud cries*] Oh, be so good,

> With sweat and with blood
> The crown to lime!

[*They handle the crown awkwardly and break it in two pieces, with which they skip about.*]

> 'Twas fate's decree!
> We speak and see!
> We hear and rhyme.

FAUST.   [*Before the mirror*] Woe's me! well-nigh distraught I feel!
MEPH.   [*Pointing to the beasts*] And even my own head almost begins to reel.
THE MONKEYS.   If good luck attend,
If fitly things blend,
Our jargon with thought
And with reason is fraught!
FAUST.   [*As above*] A flame is kindled in my breast!
Let us begone! nor linger here!
MEPH.   [*In the same position*] It now at least must be confessed,
That poets sometimes are sincere.

[*The caldron which the* SHE-MONKEY *has neglected begins to boil over; a great flame arises, which streams up the chimney. The* WITCH *comes down the chimney with horrible cries.*]

WITCH.   Ough! ough! ough! ough!
Accursed brute! accursed sow!

The caldron dost neglect, for shame!
Accursed brute to scorch the dame!

[*Perceiving* FAUST *and* MEPHISTOPHELES]

Whom have we here?
Who's sneaking here?
Whence are ye come?
With what desire?
The plague of fire
Your bones consume!

[*She dips the skimming-ladle into the caldron and throws flames at* FAUST,
MEPHISTOPHELES, *and the* MONKEYS. *The* MONKEYS *whimper.*]

MEPH. [*Twirling the whisk which he holds in his hand, and striking
among the glasses and pots*] Dash! Smash!
There lies the glass!
There lies the slime!
'Tis but a jest;
I but keep time,
Thou hellish pest,
To thine own chime!

[*While the* WITCH *steps back in rage and astonishment.*]

Dost know me! Skeleton! Vile scarecrow, thou!
Thy lord and master dost thou know?
What holds me, that I deal not now
Thee and thine apes a stunning blow?
No more respect to my red vest dost pay?
Does my cock's feather no allegiance claim?
Have I my visage masked to-day?
Must I be forced myself to name?
WITCH.   Master, forgive this rude salute!
But I perceive no cloven foot.
And your two ravens, where are they?
MEPH.   This once I must admit your plea; —
For truly I must own that we
Each other have not seen for many a day.
The culture, too, that shapes the world, at last
Hath e'en the devil in its sphere embraced;
The northern phantom from the scene hath pass'd,

Tail, talons, horns, are nowhere to be traced!
As for the foot, with which I can't dispense,
'Twould injure me in company, and hence,
Like many a youthful cavalier,
False calves I now have worn for many a year.

WITCH.   [*Dancing*] I am beside myself with joy,
To see once more the gallant Satan here!
MEPH.   Woman, no more that name employ!
WITCH.   But why? what mischief hath it done?
MEPH.   To fable-books it now doth appertain;
But people from the change have nothing won.
Rid of the evil one, the evil ones remain.
Lord Baron call thou me, so is the matter good;
Of other cavaliers the mien I wear.
Dost make no question of my gentle blood;
See here, this is the scutcheon that I bear!

[*He makes an unseemly gesture.*]

WITCH.   [*Laughing immoderately*] Ha! Ha! Just like yourself! You are, I
    ween,[2]
The same mad wag that you have ever been!
MEPH.   [*To* FAUST] My friend, learn this to understand, I pray!
To deal with witches this is still the way.
WITCH.   Now tell me, gentlemen, what you desire?
MEPH.   Of your known juice a goblet we require.
But for the very oldest let me ask;
Double its strength with years doth grow.
WITCH.   Most willingly! And here I have a flask,
From which I've sipp'd myself ere now;
What's more, it doth no longer stink;
To you a glass I joyfully will give.
[*Aside*] If unprepar'd, however, this man drink,
He hath not, as you know, an hour to live.
MEPH.   He's my good friend, with whom 'twill prosper well;
I grudge him not the choicest of thy store.
Now draw thy circle, speak thy spell,
And straight a bumper for him pour!

2. *ween*] imagine.

[*The* WITCH, *with extraordinary gestures, describes*[3] *a circle, and places strange things within it. The glasses meanwhile begin to ring, the caldron to sound, and to make music. Lastly, she brings a great book; places the* MONKEYS *in the circle to serve her as a desk, and to hold the torches. She beckons* FAUST *to approach.*]

FAUST.   [*To* MEPHISTOPHELES] Tell me, to what doth all this tend?
Where will these frantic gestures end?
This loathsome cheat, this senseless stuff
I've known and hated long enough.
MEPH.   Mere mummery, a laugh to raise!
Pray don't be so fastidious! She
But as a leech,[4] her hocus-pocus plays,
That well with you her potion may agree.

[*He compels* FAUST *to enter the circle.*]

WITCH.   [*With great emphasis, begins to declaim the book.*] This must
thou ken:[5]
Of one make ten,
Pass two, and then
Make square the three,
So rich thou'lt be.
Drop out the four!
From five and six,
Thus says the witch,
Make seven and eight.
So all is straight!
And nine is one,
And ten is none,
This is the witch's one-time-one!
FAUST.   The hag doth as in fever rave.
MEPH.   To these will follow many a stave.[6]
I know it well, so rings the book throughout;
Much time I've lost in puzzling o'er its pages,
For downright paradox, no doubt,
A mystery remains alike to fools and sages.

---

3. *describes*] traces the outline of.
4. *leech*] physician, surgeon.
5. *ken*] know, see.
6. *stave*] stanza.

Ancient the art and modern too, my friend.
'Tis still the fashion as it used to be,
Error instead of truth abroad to send
By means of three and one, and one and three.
'Tis ever taught and babbled in the schools.
Who'd take the trouble to dispute with fools?
When words men hear, in sooth, they usually believe,
That there must needs therein be something to conceive.

WITCH.   [*Continues*] The lofty power
                Of wisdom's dower,
                From all the world conceal'd!
                Who thinketh not,
                To him I wot,
                Unsought it is reveal'd.

FAUST.   What nonsense doth the hag propound?
My brain it doth well-nigh confound.
A hundred thousand fools or more,
Methinks I hear in chorus roar.

MEPH.   Incomparable Sibyl cease, I pray!
Hand us thy liquor without more delay.
And to the very brim the goblet crown!
My friend he is, and need not be afraid;
Besides, he is a man of many a grade,
Who hath drunk deep already.

[*The* WITCH, *with many ceremonies, pours the liquor into a cup; as*
            FAUST *lifts it to his mouth, a light flame arises.*]

MEPH.   Gulp it down!
No hesitation! It will prove
A cordial, and your heart inspire!
What! with the devil hand and glove,
And yet shrink back afraid of fire?

                    [*The* WITCH *dissolves the circle.* FAUST *steps out.*]

MEPH.   Now forth at once! thou dar'st not rest.
WITCH.   And much, sir, may the liquor profit you!
MEPH.   [*To the* WITCH] And if to pleasure thee I aught can do,
Pray on Walpurgis[7] mention thy request.

---

7. *Walpurgis*] On the eve of the feast day of St. Walpurgis (May Day), witches were
believed to keep an appointed rendezvous.

WITCH.   Here is a song, sung o'er, sometimes you'll see,
    That 'twill a singular effect produce.
MEPH.   [*To* FAUST] Come, quick, and let thyself be led by me;
    Thou must perspire, in order that the juice
    Thy frame may penetrate through every part.
    Then noble idleness I thee will teach to prize,
    And soon with ecstasy thou'lt recognise
    How Cupid stirs and gambols in thy heart.
FAUST.   Let me but gaze one moment in the glass!
    Too lovely was that female form!
MEPH.   Nay! nay!
    A model which all women shall surpass,
    In flesh and blood ere long thou shalt survey.
    [*Aside*] As works the draught, thou presently shalt greet
    A Helen in each woman thou dost meet.

SCENE — *A Street*

FAUST. MARGARET *passing by.*

FAUST.   Fair lady, may I thus make free
    To offer you my arm and company?
MARG.   I am no lady, am not fair,
    Can without escort home repair.

                  [*She disengages herself and exits.*]

FAUST.   By heaven! This girl is fair indeed!
    No form like hers can I recall.
    Virtue she hath, and modest heed,
    Is piquant too, and sharp withal.
    Her cheek's soft light, her rosy lips,
    No length of time will e'er eclipse!
    Her downward glance in passing by,
    Deep in my heart is stamp'd for aye;
    How curt and sharp her answer too,
    To ecstasy the feeling grew!

MEPHISTOPHELES *enters.*

FAUST.   This girl must win for me! Dost hear?
MEPH.   Which?
FAUST.   She who but now passed.
MEPH.   What! She?
    She from confession cometh here,
    From every sin absolved and free;
    I crept near the confessor's chair.
    All innocence her virgin soul,
    For next to nothing went she there;
    O'er such as she I've no control!
FAUST.   She's past fourteen.
MEPH.   You really talk
    Like any gay Lothario,
    Who every floweret from its stalk
    Would pluck, and deems nor grace, nor truth,
    Secure against his arts, forsooth!
    This ne'er the less won't always do.
FAUST.   Sir Moralizer, prithee, pause;
    Nor plague me with your tiresome laws!
    To cut the matter short, my friend,
    She must this very night be mine, —
    And if to help me you decline,
    Midnight shall see our compact end.
MEPH.   What may occur just bear in mind!
    A fortnight's space, at least, I need,
    A fit occasion but to find.
FAUST.   With but seven hours I could succeed;
    Nor should I want the devil's wile,
    So young a creature to beguile.
MEPH.   Like any Frenchman now you speak,
    But do not fret, I pray; why seek
    To hurry to enjoyment straight?
    The pleasure is not half so great,
    As when at first around, above,
    With all the fooleries of love,
    The puppet you can knead and mould
    As in Italian story oft is told.
FAUST.   No such incentives do I need.
MEPH.   But now, without offense or jest!
    You cannot quickly, I protest,
    In winning this sweet child succeed.

> By storm we cannot take the fort,
> To stratagem we must resort.

FAUST.   Conduct me to her place of rest!
> Some token of the angel bring!
> A kerchief from her snowy breast,
> A garter bring me, — any thing!

MEPH.   That I my anxious zeal may prove,
> Your pangs to sooth and aid your love,
> A single moment will we not delay,
> Will lead you to her room this very day.

FAUST.   And shall I see her? — Have her?

MEPH.   No!
> She to a neighbour's house will go;
> But in her atmosphere alone,
> The tedious hours meanwhile you may employ,
> In blissful dreams of future joy.

FAUST.   Can we go now?

MEPH.   'Tis yet too soon.

FAUST.   Some present for my love procure!   [*Exit.*]

MEPH.   Presents so soon! 'tis well! success is sure!
> Full many a goodly place I know,
> And treasures buried long ago;
> I must a bit o'erlook them now.   [*Exit.*]

SCENE — *Evening — A Small and Neat Room*

MARG.   [*Braiding and binding up her hair*] I would give something
>   now to know,
> Who yonder gentleman could be!
> He had a gallant air, I trow,
> And doubtless was of high degree:
> That written on his brow was seen —
> Nor else would he so bold have been.   [*Exit.*]

MEPH.   Come in! tread softly! be discreet!

FAUST.   [*After a pause*] Begone and leave me, I entreat!

MEPH.   [*Looking round*] Not every maiden is so neat.   [*Exit.*]

FAUST.   [*Gazing round*] Welcome sweet twilight, calm and blest,
> That in this hallow'd precinct reigns!
> Fond yearning love, inspire my breast,

Feeding on hope's sweet dew thy blissful pains!
What stillness here environs me!
Content and order brood around.
What fulness in this poverty!
In this small cell what bliss profound!

[*He throws himself on the leather arm-chair beside the bed.*]

Receive me thou, who hast in thine embrace,
Welcom'd in joy and grief the ages flown!
How oft the children of a by-gone race
Have cluster'd round this patriarchal throne!
Haply she, also, whom I hold so dear,
For Christmas gift, with grateful joy possess'd,
Hath with the full round cheek of childhood, here,
Her grandsire's wither'd hand devoutly press'd.
Maiden! I feel thy spirit haunt the place,
Breathing of order and abounding grace.
As with a mother's voice it prompteth thee,
The pure white cover o'er the board to spread,
To strew the crisping sand beneath thy tread.
Dear hand! so godlike in its ministry!
The hut becomes a paradise through thee!
And here —   [*He raises the bed-curtain.*]
How thrills my pulse with strange delight!
Here could I linger hours untold;
Thou, Nature, didst in vision bright,
The embryo angel here unfold.
Here lay the child, her bosom warm
With life; while steeped in slumber's dew,
To perfect grace, her godlike form,
With pure and hallow'd weavings grew!

And thou! ah here what seekest thou?
How quails mine inmost being now!
What wouldst thou here? what makes thy heart so sore?
Unhappy Faust! I know thee now no more.

Do I a magic atmosphere inhale?
Erewhile, my passion would not brook delay!
Now in a pure love-dream I melt away.
Are we the sport of every passing gale?

Should she return and enter now,

How wouldst thou rue thy guilty flame!
Proud vaunter — thou wouldst hide thy brow, —
And at her feet sink down with shame.

MEPH.   Quick! quick! below I see her there.

FAUST.   Away! I will return no more!

MEPH.   Here is a casket, with a store
        Of jewels, which I got elsewhere;
        Just lay it in the press; make haste!
        I swear to you, 'twill turn her brain;
        Therein some trifles I have placed,
        Wherewith another to obtain.
        But child is child, and play is play.

FAUST.   I know not — shall I?

MEPH.   Do you ask?
Perchance you would retain the treasure?
If such your wish, why then, I say,
Henceforth absolve me from my task,
Nor longer waste your hours of leisure.
I trust you're not by avarice led!
I rub my hands, I scratch my head, —

[*He places the casket in the press and closes the lock.*]

Now quick! Away!
That soon the sweet young creature may
The wish and purpose of your heart obey;
Yet stand you there
As would you to the lecture-room repair,
As if before you stood,
Arrayed in flesh and blood,
Physics and metaphysics weird and grey! —
Away!   [*Exeunt.*]

MARG.   [*With a lamp*] Here 'tis so close, so sultry now,

[*She opens the window.*]

Yet out of doors 'tis not so warm.
I feel so strange, I know not how —
I wish my mother would come home.
Through me there runs a shuddering —
I'm but a foolish timid thing!

[*While undressing herself she begins to sing.*]

There was a king in Thule,
True even to the grave;
To whom his dying mistress
A golden beaker gave.

At every feast he drained it,
Naught was to him so dear,
And often as he drained it,
Gush'd from his eyes the tear.

When death came, unrepining
His cities o'er he told;
All to his heir resigning,
Except his cup of gold.

With many a knightly vassal
At a royal feast sat he,
In yon proud hall ancestral,
In his castle o'er the sea.

Up stood the jovial monarch,
And quaff'd his last life's glow,
Then hurled the hallow'd goblet
Into the flood below.

He saw it splashing, drinking,
And plunging in the sea;
His eyes meanwhile were sinking,
And never again drank he.

[*She opens the press to put away her clothes, and perceives the casket.*]

How comes this lovely casket here? The press
I locked, of that I'm confident.
'Tis very wonderful! What's in it I can't guess;
Perhaps 'twas brought by some one in distress,
And left in pledge for loan my mother lent.
Here by a ribbon hangs a little key!
I have a mind to open it and see!
Heavens! only look! what have we here!
In all my days ne'er saw I such a sight!
Jewels! which any noble dame might wear,

For some high pageant richly dight![1]
This chain — how would it look on me!
These splendid gems, whose may they be?

[*She puts them on and steps before the glass.*]

Were but the ear-rings only mine!
Thus one has quite another air.
What boots it to be young and fair?
It doubtless may be very fine;
But then, alas, none cares for you,
And praise sounds half like pity too.
Gold all doth lure,
Gold doth secure
All things. Alas, we poor!

SCENE — *Promenade*

FAUST *walking thoughtfully up and down. To him* MEPHISTOPHELES.

MEPH.   By all rejected love! By hellish fire I curse,
         Would I knew aught to make my imprecation worse!
FAUST.   What aileth thee? what chafes thee now so sore?
         A face like that I never saw before!
MEPH.   I'd yield me to the devil instantly,
         Did it not happen that myself am he!
FAUST.   There must be some disorder in thy wit!
         To rave thus like a madman, is it fit?
MEPH.   Think! only think! The gems for Gretchen[1] brought,
         Them hath a priest now made his own! —
         A glimpse of them the mother caught,
         And 'gan with secret fear to groan.
         The woman's scent is keen enough;
         Doth ever in the prayer-book snuff;
         Smells every article to ascertain
         Whether the thing is holy or profane,
         And scented in the jewels rare,

1. *dight*] dressed, adorned.

1. *Gretchen*] the German diminutive of Marguerite (Margaret); literally, "little Marguerite."

That there was not much blessing there.
"My child," she cries, "ill-gotten good
Ensnares the soul, consumes the blood;
With them we'll deck our Lady's shrine,
She'll cheer our souls with bread divine!"
At this poor Gretchen 'gan to pout;
'Tis a gift-horse, at least, she thought,
And sure, he godless cannot be,
Who brought them here so cleverly.
Straight for a priest the mother sent,
Who, when he understood the jest,
With what he saw was well content.
"This shows a pious mind!" Quoth he:
"Self-conquest is true victory.
The Church hath a good stomach, she, with zest,
Whole countries hath swallow'd down,
And never yet a surfeit known.
The Church alone, be it confessed,
Daughters, can ill-got wealth digest."

FAUST.   It is a general custom, too.
Practised alike by king and Jew.

MEPH.   With that, clasp, chain, and ring, he swept
As they were mushrooms; and the casket,
Without one word of thanks, he kept,
As if of nuts it were a basket.
Promised reward in heaven, then forth he hied—
And greatly they were edified.

FAUST.   And Gretchen?

MEPH.   In unquiet mood
Knows neither what she would or should;
The trinkets night and day thinks o'er,
On him who brought them, dwells still more.

FAUST.   The darling's sorrow grieves me, bring
Another set without delay!
The first, methinks, was no great thing.

MEPH.   All's to my gentleman child's play!

FAUST.   Plan all things to achieve my end!
Engage the attention of her friend!
No milk-and-water devil be,
And bring fresh jewels instantly!   [*Exit.*]

MEPH.   Your doting love-sick fool, with ease,
    Merely his lady-love to please,
    Sun, moon, and stars in sport would puff away.   *[Exit.]*

SCENE — *The Neighbour's House*

MARTHA.   *[Alone]* God pardon my dear husband, he
    Doth not in truth act well by me!
    Forth in the world abroad to roam,
    And leave me on the straw at home.
    And yet his will I ne'er did thwart,
    God knows, I lov'd him from my heart.   *[She weeps.]*
    Perchance he's dead! — oh wretched state! —
    Had I but a certificate!

MARGARET *comes.*

MARG.   Dame Martha!
MARTHA.   Gretchen?
MARG.   Only think!
    My knees beneath me well-nigh sink!
    Within my press I've found to-day,
    Another case, of ebony.
    And things — magnificent they are,
    More costly than the first, by far.
MARTHA.   You must not name it to your mother!
    It would to shrift,[1] just like the other.
MARG.   Nay look at them! now only see!
MARTHA.   *[Dresses her up]*. Thou happy creature!
MARG.   Woe is me!
    Them in the street I cannot wear,
    Or in the church, or any where.
MARTHA.   Come often over here to me,
    The gems put on quite privately;

---

1. *shrift*] confession made to a priest. In other words, the jewels would be taken by the
priest as a token of penitence.

And then before the mirror walk an hour or so,
Thus we shall have our pleasure too.
Then suitable occasions we must seize,
As at a feast, to show them by degrees:
A chain at first, pearl ear-drops then, — your mother
Won't see them, or we'll coin some tale or other.

MARG.   But, who, I wonder, could the caskets bring?
I fear there's something wrong about the thing!   [A knock.]
Good heavens! can that my mother be?

MARTHA.   [Peering through the blind] 'Tis a strange gentleman, I see.
Come in!

MEPHISTOPHELES enters.

MEPH.   I've ventur'd to intrude to-day.
Ladies, excuse the liberty, I pray.

[He steps back respectfully before MARGARET.]

After dame Martha Schwerdtlein I inquire!

MARTHA.   'Tis I. Pray what have you to say to me?

MEPH.   [Aside to her] I know you now, — and therefore will retire;
At present you've distinguished company.
Pardon the freedom, Madam, with your leave,
I will make free to call again at eve.

MARTHA.   [Aloud] Why, child, of all strange notions, he
For some grand lady taketh thee!

MARG.   I am, in truth, of humble blood —
The gentleman is far too good —
Nor gems nor trinkets are my own.

MEPH.   Oh 'tis not the mere ornaments alone;
Her glance and mien far more betray.
Rejoiced I am that I may stay.

MARTHA.   Your business, Sir? I long to know —

MEPH.   Would I could happier tidings show!
I trust mine errand you'll not let me rue;
Your husband's dead, and greeteth you.

MARTHA.   Is dead? True heart! Oh misery!
My husband dead! Oh, I shall die!

MARG.   Alas! good Martha! don't despair!

MEPH.   Now listen to the sad affair!

MARG.   I for this cause should fear to love.
    The loss my certain death would prove.
MEPH.   Joy still must sorrow, sorrow joy attend.
MARTHA.   Proceed, and tell the story of his end!
MEPH.   At Padua, in St. Anthony's,
    In holy ground his body lies;
    Quiet and cool his place of rest,
    With pious ceremonials blest.
MARTHA.   And had you naught besides to bring?
MEPH.   Oh yes! one grave and solemn prayer;
    Let them for him three hundred masses sing!
    But in my pockets, I have nothing there.
MARTHA.   No trinket! no love-token did he send!
    What every journeyman safe in his pouch will hoard
    There for remembrance fondly stored,
    And rather hungers, rather begs than spend!
MEPH.   Madam, in truth, it grieves me sore,
    But he his gold not lavishly hath spent.
    His failings too he deeply did repent,
    Ay! and his evil plight bewail'd still more.
MARG.   Alas! That men should thus be doomed to woe!
    I for his soul will many a requiem pray.
MEPH.   A husband you deserve this very day;
    A child so worthy to be loved.
MARG.   Ah no,
    That time hath not yet come for me.
MEPH.   If not a spouse, a gallant let it be.
    Among heaven's choicest gifts, I place,
    So sweet a darling to embrace.
MARG.   Our land doth no such usage know.
MEPH.   Usage or not, it happens so.
MARTHA.   Go on, I pray!
MEPH.   I stood by his bedside.
    Something less foul it was than dung;
    'Twas straw half rotten; yet, he as a Christian died.
    And sorely hath remorse his conscience wrung.
    "Wretch that I was," quoth he, with parting breath,
    "So to forsake my business and my wife!
    Ah! the remembrance is my death,
    Could I but have her pardon in this life!" —
MARTHA.   [*Weeping*] Dear soul! I've long forgiven him, indeed!

MEPH.   "Though she, God knows, was more to blame than I."
MARTHA.   He lied! What, on the brink of death to lie!
MEPH.   If I am skill'd the countenance to read,
    He doubtless fabled as he parted hence. —
    "No time had I to gape, or take my ease," he said,
    "First to get children, and then get them bread;
    And bread, too, in the very widest sense;
    Nor could I eat in peace even my proper share."
MARTHA.   What, all my truth, my love forgotten quite?
    My weary drudgery by day and night!
MEPH.   Not so! He thought of you with tender care.
    Quoth he: "Heaven knows how fervently I prayed,
    For wife and children when from Malta bound; —
    The prayer hath heaven with favour crowned;
    We took a Turkish vessel which conveyed
    Rich store of treasure for the Sultan's court;
    Its own reward our gallant action brought;
    The captur'd prize was shared among the crew
    And of the treasure I received my due."
MARTHA.   How? Where? The treasure hath he buried, pray?
MEPH.   Where the four winds have blown it, who can say?
    In Naples as he stroll'd, a stranger there, —
    A comely maid took pity on my friend;
    And gave such tokens of her love and care,
    That he retained them to his blessed end.
MARTHA.   Scoundrel! to rob his children of their bread!
    And all this misery, this bitter need,
    Could not his course of recklessness impede!
MEPH.   Well, he hath paid the forfeit, and is dead.
    Now were I in your place, my counsel hear;
    My weeds[2] I'd wear for one chaste year,
    And for another lover meanwhile would look out.
MARTHA.   Alas, I might search far and near,
    Not quickly should I find another like my first!
    There could not be a fonder fool than mine,
    Only he loved too well abroad to roam;
    Loved foreign women too, and foreign wine,
    And loved besides the dice accurs'd.

2. *weeds*] garments; in this case widow's mourning garments.

MEPH.   All had gone swimmingly, no doubt,
　　　　Had he but given you at home,
　　　　On his side, just as wide a range.
　　　　Upon such terms, to you I swear,
　　　　Myself with you would gladly rings exchange!
MARTHA.   The gentleman is surely pleas'd to jest!
MEPH.   [*Aside*] Now to be off in time, were best!
　　　　She'd make the very devil marry her.
　　　　[*To* MARGARET] How fares it with your heart?
MARG.   How mean you, Sir?
MEPH.   [*Aside*] The sweet young innocent!
　　　　[*Aloud*] Ladies, farewell!
MARG.   Farewell!
MARTHA.   But ere you leave us, quickly tell!
　　　　I from a witness fain had heard,
　　　　Where, how, and when my husband died and was interr'd.
　　　　To forms I've always been attached indeed,
　　　　His death I fain would in the journals read.
MEPH.   Ay, madam, what two witnesses declare
　　　　Is held as valid everywhere;
　　　　A gallant friend I have, not far from here,
　　　　Who will for you before the judge appear.
　　　　I'll bring him straight.
MARTHA.   I pray you do!
MEPH.   And this young lady, we shall find her too?
　　　　A noble youth, far travelled, he
　　　　Shows to the sex all courtesy.
MARG.   I in his presence needs must blush for shame.
MEPH.   Not in the presence of a crowned king!
MARTHA.   The garden, then, behind my house, we'll name,
　　　　There we'll await you both this evening.

SCENE—*A Street*

FAUST, MEPHISTOPHELES.

FAUST.   How is it now? How speeds it? Is't in train?
MEPH.   Bravo! I find you all aflame!

Gretchen full soon your own you'll name.
This eve, at neighbour Martha's, her you'll meet again;
The woman seems expressly made
To drive the pimp and gipsy's trade.

FAUST.   Good!

MEPH.   But from us she something would request.

FAUST.   A favour claims return as this world goes.

MEPH.   We have on oath but duly to attest,
    That her dead husband's limbs, outstretch'd, repose
    In holy ground at Padua.

FAUST.   Sage indeed!
    So I suppose we straight must journey there!

MEPH.   *Sancta simplicitas!* For that no need!
    Without much knowledge we have but to swear.

FAUST.   If you have nothing better to suggest,
    Against your plan I must at once protest.

MEPH.   Oh, holy man! methinks I have you there!
    In all your life say, have you ne'er
    False witness borne, until this hour?
    Have you of God, the world, and all it doth contain,
    Of man, and that which worketh in his heart and brain,
    Not definitions given, in words of weight and power,
    With front unblushing, and a dauntless breast?
    Yet, if into the depth of things you go,
    Touching these matters, it must be confess'd,
    As much as of Herr Schwerdtlein's death you know!

FAUST.   Thou art and dost remain liar and sophist too.

MEPH.   Ay, if one did not take a somewhat deeper view!
    To-morrow, in all honour, thou
    Poor Gretchen wilt befool, and vow
    Thy soul's deep love, in lover's fashion.

FAUST.   And from my heart.

MEPH.   All good and fair!
    Then deathless constancy thou'lt swear;
    Speak of one all o'ermastering passion, —
    Will that too issue from the heart?

FAUST.   Forbear!
    When passion sways me, and I seek to frame
    Fit utterance for feeling, deep, intense,
    And for my frenzy finding no fit name,
    Sweep round the ample world with every sense,

> Grasp at the loftiest words to speak my flame,
> And call the glow, wherewith I burn,
> Quenchless, eternal, yea, eterne —
> Is that of sophistry a devilish play?

MEPH.   Yet am I right!

FAUST.   Mark this, my friend,
> And spare my lungs; who would the right maintain,
> And hath a tongue wherewith his point to gain,
> Will gain it in the end.
> But come, of gossip I am weary quite;
> Because I've no resource, thou'rt in the right.

SCENE — *Garden*

MARGARET *on* FAUST's *arm.* MARTHA *with* MEPHISTOPHELES *walking up and down.*

MARG.   I feel it, you but spare my ignorance,
> The gentleman to shame me stoops thus low.
> A traveller from complaisance,
> Still makes the best of things; I know
> Too well, my humble prattle never can
> Have power to entertain so wise a man.

FAUST.   One glance, one word from thee doth charm me more,
> Than the world's wisdom or the sage's lore.

[He kisses her hand.]

MARG.   Nay! trouble not yourself! A hand so coarse,
> So rude as mine, how can you kiss!
> What constant work at home must I not do perforce!
> My mother too exacting is.

[They pass on.]

MARTHA.   Thus, sir, unceasing travel is your lot?

MEPH.   Traffic and duty urge us! With what pain
> Are we compelled to leave full many a spot,
> Where yet we dare not once remain!

MARTHA.   In youth's wild years, with vigour crown'd,
> 'Tis not amiss thus through the world to sweep;

But ah, the evil days come round!
And to a lonely grave as bachelor to creep,
A pleasant thing has no one found.
MEPH.　The prospect fills me with dismay.
MARTHA.　Therefore in time, dear sir, reflect, I pray.

[*They pass on.*]

MARG.　Ay, out of sight is out of mind!
　　　Politeness easy is to you;
　　　Friends everywhere, and not a few,
　　　Wiser than I am, you will find.
FAUST.　O dearest, trust me, what doth pass for sense
　　　Full oft is self-conceit and blindness!
MARG.　　　　　　　　　　　　How?
FAUST.　Simplicity and holy innocence, —
　　　When will ye learn your hallow'd worth to know!
　　　Ah, when will meekness and humility,
　　　Kind and all-bounteous nature's loftiest dower —
MARG.　Only one little moment think of me!
　　　To think of you I shall have many an hour.
FAUST.　You are perhaps much alone?
MARG.　Yes, small our household is, I own,
　　　Yet must I see to it. No maid we keep,
　　　And I must cook, sew, knit, and sweep,
　　　Still early on my feet and late;
　　　My mother is in all things, great and small,
　　　So accurate!
　　　Not that for thrift there is such pressing need;
　　　Than others we might make more show indeed:
　　　My father left behind a small estate,
　　　A house and garden near the city-wall.
　　　But fairly quiet now my days, I own;
　　　As soldier is my brother gone;
　　　My little sister's dead; the babe to rear
　　　Occasion'd me some care and fond annoy;
　　　But I would go through all again with joy,
　　　The darling was to me so dear.
FAUST.　An angel, sweet, if it resembled thee!
MARG.　I reared it up, and it grew fond of me.
　　　After my father's death it saw the day;
　　　We gave my mother up for lost, she lay

In such a wretched plight, and then at length
So very slowly she regain'd her strength.
Weak as she was, 'twas vain for her to try
Herself to suckle the poor babe, so I
Reared it on milk and water all alone;
And thus the child became as 'twere my own;
Within my arms it stretched itself and grew,
And smiling, nestled in my bosom too.

FAUST.   Doubtless the purest happiness was thine.

MARG.   But many weary hours, in sooth, were also mine.
At night its little cradle stood
Close to my bed; so was I wide awake
If it but stirred;
One while I was obliged to give it food,
Or to my arms the darling take;
From bed full oft must rise, whene'er its cry I heard,
And, dancing it, must pace the chamber to and fro;
Stand at the wash-tub early; forthwith go
To market, and then mind the cooking too —
To-morrow like to-day, the whole year through.
Ah, sir, thus living, it must be confess'd
One's spirits are not always of the best;
Yet it a relish gives to food and rest.

[*They pass on.*]

MARTHA.   Poor women! we are badly off, I own;
A bachelor's conversion's hard, indeed!

MEPH.   Madam, with one like you it rests alone,
To tutor me a better course to lead.

MARTHA.   Speak frankly, sir, none is there you have met?
Has your heart ne'er attach'd itself as yet?

MEPH.   One's own fire-side and a good wife are gold
And pearls of price, so says the proverb old.

MARTHA.   I mean, has passion never stirred your breast?

MEPH.   I've everywhere been well received, I own.

MARTHA.   Yet hath your heart no earnest preference known?

MEPH.   With ladies one should ne'er presume to jest.

MARTHA.   Ah! you mistake!

MEPH.   I'm sorry I'm so blind!
But this I know — that you are very kind.

[*They pass on.*]

FAUST.   Me, little angel, didst thou recognise,

When in the garden first I came?

MARG.   Did you not see it? I cast down my eyes.

FAUST.   Thou dost forgive my boldness, dost not blame
The liberty I took that day,
When thou from church didst lately wend thy way?

MARG.   I was confused. So had it never been;
No one of me could any evil say.
Alas, thought I, he doubtless in thy mien,
Something unmaidenly or bold hath seen?
It seemed as if it struck him suddenly,
Here's just a girl with whom one may make free!
Yet I must own that then I scarcely knew
What in your favour here began at once to plead;
Yet I was angry with myself indeed,
That I more angry could not feel with you.

FAUST.   Sweet love!

MARG.   Just wait awhile!

[*She gathers a star-flower and plucks off the leaves one after another.*]

FAUST.   A nosegay may that be?

MARG.   No! It is but a game.

FAUST.   How?

MARG.   Go, you'll laugh at me!

[*She plucks off the leaves and murmurs to herself.*]

FAUST.   What murmurest thou?

MARG.   [*Half aloud*] He loves me — loves me not.

FAUST.   Sweet angel, with thy face of heavenly bliss!

MARG.   [*Continues*] He loves me — not — he loves me — not —

[*Plucking off the last leaf with fond joy.*]

He loves me!

FAUST.   Yes!

And this flower-language, darling, let it be,
A heavenly oracle! He loveth thee!
Know'st thou the meaning of, He loveth thee?

[*He seizes both her hands.*]

MARG.   I tremble so!

FAUST.   Nay! Do not tremble, love!
Let this hand-pressure, let this glance reveal

Feelings, all power of speech above;
To give oneself up wholly and to feel
A joy that must eternal prove!
Eternal! — Yes, its end would be despair.
No end! — It cannot end!

[MARGARET *presses his hand, extricates herself, and runs away. He stands
a moment in thought and then follows her.*]

MARTHA.   [*Approaching*] Night's closing.
MEPH.   Yes, we'll presently away.
MARTHA.   I would entreat you longer yet to stay;
But 'tis a wicked place, just here about;
It is as if the folk had nothing else to do,
Nothing to think of too,
But gaping watch their neighbours, who goes in and out;
And scandal's busy still, do whatsoe'er one may.
And our young couple?
MEPH.   They have flown up there.
The wanton butterflies!
MARTHA.   He seems to take to her.
MEPH.   And she to him. 'Tis of the world the way!

SCENE — A *Summer-House*

MARGARET *runs in, hides behind the door, holds the tip of her finger
to her lips, and peeps through the crevice.*

MARG.   He comes!
FAUST.   Ah, little rogue so thou
Think'st to provoke me! I have caught thee now!

[*He kisses her.*]

MARG.   [*Embracing him, and returning the kiss*] Dearest of men! I love
thee from my heart!

[MEPHISTOPHELES *knocks.*]

FAUST.   [*Stamping*] Who's there?
MEPH.   A friend!
FAUST.   A brute!

MEPH.   'Tis time to part.
MARTHA.   [*Comes*] Ay, it is late, good sir.
FAUST.   Mayn't I attend you, then?
MARG.   Oh no — my mother would — adieu, adieu!
FAUST.   And must I really then take leave of you?
     Farewell!
MARTHA.   Good-bye!
MARG.   Ere long to meet again!

                    [*Exeunt* FAUST *and* MEPHISTOPHELES.]

MARG.   Good heavens! how all things far and near
     Must fill his mind, — a man like this!
     Abash'd before him I appear,
     And say to all things only, yes.
     Poor simple child, I cannot see,
     What 'tis that he can find in me.   [*Exit.*]

               SCENE — *Forest and Cavern*

FAUST.   [*Alone*] Spirit sublime! Thou gav'st me, gav'st me all
     For which I prayed! Not vainly hast thou turn'd
     To me thy countenance in flaming fire:
     Gavest me glorious nature for my realm,
     And also power to feel her and enjoy;
     Not merely with a cold and wondering glance,
     Thou dost permit me in her depths profound,
     As in the bosom of a friend to gaze.
     Before me thou dost lead her living tribes,
     And dost in silent grove, in air and stream
     Teach me to know my kindred. And when roars
     The howling storm-blast through the groaning wood,
     Wrenching the giant pine, which in its fall
     Crashing sweeps down its neighbour trunks and boughs,
     While hollow thunder from the hill resounds;
     Then thou dost lead me to some shelter'd cave,
     Dost there reveal me to myself, and show
     Of my own bosom the mysterious depths.
     And when with soothing beam, the moon's pale orb

Full in my view climbs up the pathless sky,
From crag and dewy grove, the silvery forms
Of by-gone ages hover, and assuage
The joy austere of contemplative thought.

Oh, that naught perfect is assign'd to man,
I feel, alas! With this exalted joy,
Which lifts me near and nearer to the gods,
Thou gav'st me this companion, unto whom
I needs must cling, though cold and insolent,
He still degrades me to myself, and turns
Thy glorious gifts to nothing, with a breath.
He in my bosom with malicious zeal
For that fair image fans a raging fire;
From craving to enjoyment thus I reel,
And in enjoyment languish for desire.

MEPHISTOPHELES *enters.*

MEPH.   Of this lone life have you not had your fill?
         How for so long can it have charms for you?
         'Tis well enough to try it if you will;
         But then away again to something new!
FAUST.   Would you could better occupy your leisure,
         Than in disturbing thus my hours of joy.
MEPH.   Well! Well! I'll leave you to yourself with pleasure,
         A serious tone you hardly dare employ.
         To part from one so crazy, harsh, and cross,
         Were not in truth a grievous loss.
         The live-long day, for you I toil and fret;
         Ne'er from his worship's face a hint I get,
         What pleases him, or what to let alone.
FAUST.   Ay truly! that is just the proper tone!
         He wearies me, and would with thanks be paid!
MEPH.   Poor Son of Earth, without my aid,
         How would thy weary days have flown?
         Thee of thy foolish whims I've cured,
         Thy vain imaginations banished,
         And but for me, be well assured,
         Thou from this sphere must soon have vanished.
         In rocky hollows and in caverns drear,

Why like an owl sit moping here?
Wherefore from dripping stones and moss with ooze embued,
Dost suck, like any toad, thy food?
A rare, sweet pastime. Verily!
The doctor cleaveth still to thee.

FAUST.   Dost comprehend what bliss without alloy
From this wild wand'ring in the desert springs? —
Couldst thou but guess the new life-power it brings,
Thou wouldst be fiend enough to envy me my joy.

MEPH.   What super-earthly ecstasy! at night,
To lie in darkness on the dewy height,
Embracing heaven and earth in rapture high,
The soul dilating to a deity;
With prescient yearnings pierce the core of earth,
Feel in your labouring breast the six-days' birth,
Enjoy, in proud delight what no one knows,
While your love-rapture o'er creation flows, —
The earthly lost in beatific vision,
And then the lofty intuition —   [*With a gesture.*]
I need not tell you how — to close!

FAUST.   Fie on you!

MEPH.   This displeases you? "For shame!"
You are forsooth entitled to exclaim;
We to chaste ears it seems must not pronounce
What, nathless, the chaste heart cannot renounce.
Well, to be brief, the joy as fit occasions rise,
I grudge you not, of specious lies.
But long this mood thou'lt not retain.
Already thou'rt again outworn,
And should this last, thou wilt be torn
By frenzy or remorse and pain.
Enough of this! Thy true love dwells apart,
And all to her seems flat and tame;
Alone thine image fills her heart,
She loves thee with an all-devouring flame.
First came thy passion with o'erpowering rush,
Like mountain torrent, swollen by the melted snow;
Full in her heart didst pour the sudden gush,
Now has thy brooklet ceased to flow.
Instead of sitting throned midst forests wild,

It would become so great a lord
To comfort the enamour'd child,
And the young monkey for her love reward.
To her the hours seem miserably long;
She from the window sees the clouds float by
As o'er the lofty city-walls they fly,
"If I a birdie were!" so runs her song,
Half through the night and all day long.
Cheerful sometimes, more oft at heart full sore;
Fairly outwept seem now her tears,
Anon she tranquil is, or so appears,
And love-sick evermore.

FAUST.   Snake! Serpent vile!

MEPH.   [*Aside*] Good! If I catch thee with my guile!

FAUST.   Vile reprobate! go get thee hence;
Forbear the lovely girl to name!
Nor in my half-distracted sense,
Kindle anew the smouldering flame!

MEPH.   What wouldest thou! She thinks you've taken flight;
It seems, she's partly in the right.

FAUST.   I'm near her still — and should I distant rove,
Her I can ne'er forget, ne'er lose her love;
And all things touch'd by those sweet lips of hers,
Even the very Host, my envy stirs.

MEPH.   'Tis well! I oft have envied you indeed,
The twin-pair that among the roses feed.

FAUST.   Pander, avaunt!

MEPH.   Go to! I laugh, the while you rail,
The power which fashion'd youth and maid,
Well understood the noble trade;
So neither shall occasion fail.
But hence! — A mighty grief I trow!
Unto thy lov'd one's chamber thou
And not to death shouldst go.

FAUST.   What is to me heaven's joy within her arms?
What though my life her bosom warms! —
Do I not ever feel her woe?
The outcast am I not, unhoused, unblest,
Inhuman monster, without aim or rest,
Who, like the greedy surge, from rock to rock,
Sweeps down the dread abyss with desperate shock?

While she, within her lowly cot, which graced
The Alpine slope, beside the waters wild,
Her homely cares in that small world embraced,
Secluded lived, a simple, artless child.
Was't not enough, in thy delirious whirl
To blast the steadfast rocks;
Her, and her peace as well,
Must I, God-hated one, to ruin hurl!
Dost claim this holocaust, remorseless Hell!
Fiend, help me to cut short the hours of dread!
Let what must happen, happen speedily!
Her direful doom fall crushing on my head,
And into ruin let her plunge with me!

MEPH. Why how again it seethes and glows!
Away, thou fool! Her torment ease!
When such a head no issue sees,
It pictures straight the final close.
Long life to him who boldly dares!
A devil's pluck thou'rt wont to show;
As for a devil who despairs,
Nothing I find so mawkish here below.

SCENE — *Margaret's Room*

MARG. [*Alone at her spinning wheel*]

My peace is gone,
    My heart is sore,
I find it never,
    And nevermore!

Where him I have not,
    Is the grave; and all
The world to me
    Is turned to gall.

My wilder'd brain
    Is overwrought;
My feeble senses
    Are distraught.

My peace is gone,
  My heart is sore,
I find it never,
  And nevermore!

For him from the window
  I gaze, at home;
For him and him only
  Abroad I roam.

His lofty step,
  His bearing high,
The smile of his lip,
  The power of his eye,

His witching words,
  Their tones of bliss,
His hand's fond pressure,
  And ah—his kiss!

My peace is gone,
  My heart is sore,
I find it never,
  And nevermore.

My bosom aches
  To feel him near;
Ah, could I clasp
  And fold him here!

Kiss him and kiss him
  Again would I,
And on his kisses
  I fain would die.

SCENE—*Martha's Garden*

MARGARET *and* FAUST.

MARG.   Promise me, Henry!
FAUST.   What I can!
MARG.   How thy religion fares, I fain would hear.

Thou art a good kind-hearted man,
Only that way not well-disposed, I fear.
FAUST.   Forbear, my child! Thou feelest thee I love;
My heart, my blood I'd give, my love to prove,
And none would of their faith or church bereave.
MARG.   That's not enough, we must ourselves believe!
FAUST.   Must we?
MARG.   Ah, could I but thy soul inspire!
Thou honourest not the sacraments, alas!
FAUST.   I honour them.
MARG.   But yet without desire;
'Tis long since thou hast been either to shrift or mass.
Dost thou believe in God?
FAUST.   My darling, who dares say,
Yes, I in God believe?
Question or priest or sage, and they
Seem, in the answer you receive,
To mock the questioner.
MARG.   Then thou dost not believe?
FAUST.   Sweet one! my meaning do not misconceive!
Him who dare name?
And who proclaim,
Him I believe?
Who that can feel,
His heart can steel,
To say: I believe him not?
The All-embracer,
All-sustainer,
Holds and sustains he not
Thee, me, himself?
Lifts not the Heaven its dome above?
Doth not the firm-set earth beneath us lie?
And beaming tenderly with looks of love,
Climb not the everlasting stars on high?
Do we not gaze into each other's eyes?
Nature's impenetrable agencies,
Are they not thronging on thy heart and brain,
Viewless, or visible to mortal ken,
Around thee weaving their mysterious chain?
Fill thence thy heart, how large soe'er it be;
And in the feeling when thou utterly art blest,

Then call it, what thou wilt,—
Call it Bliss! Heart! Love! God!
I have no name for it!
'Tis feeling all;
Name is but sound and smoke
Shrouding the glow of heaven.

MARG.   All this is doubtless good and fair;
Almost the same the parson says,
Only in slightly different phrase.

FAUST.   Beneath Heaven's sunshine, everywhere,
This is the utterance of the human heart;
Each in his language doth the like impart;
Then why not I in mine?

MARG.   What thus I hear
Sounds plausible, yet I'm not reconciled;
There's something wrong about it; much I fear
That thou art not a Christian.

FAUST.   My sweet child!

MARG.   Alas! it long hath sorely troubled me,
To see thee in such odious company.

FAUST.   How so?

MARG.   The man who comes with thee, I hate,
Yea, in my spirit's inmost depths abhor;
As his loath'd visage, in my life before,
Naught to my heart e'er gave a pang so great.

FAUST.   Him fear not, my sweet love!

MARG.   His presence chills my blood.
Towards all beside I have a kindly mood;
Yet, though I yearn to gaze on thee, I feel
At sight of him strange horror o'er me steal;
That he's a villain my conviction's strong.
May Heaven forgive me, if I do him wrong!

FAUST.   Yet such strange fellows in the world must be!

MARG.   I would not live with such an one as he.
If for a moment he but enter here,
He looks around him with a mocking sneer,
And malice ill-conceal'd;
That he with naught on earth can sympathize is clear
Upon his brow 'tis legibly revealed,
That to his heart no living soul is dear.
So blest I feel, within thine arms,

So warm and happy, — free from all alarms;
And still my heart doth close when he comes near.
FAUST.   Foreboding angel! check thy fear!
MARG.   It so o'ermasters me, that when,
        Or wheresoe'er, his step I hear,
        I almost think, no more I love thee then.
        Besides, when he is near, I ne'er could pray.
        This eats into my heart; with thee
        The same, my Henry, it must be.
FAUST.   This is antipathy!
MARG.   I must away.
FAUST.   For one brief hour then may I never rest,
        And heart to heart, and soul to soul be pressed?
MARG.   Ah, if I slept alone! To-night
        The bolt I fain would leave undrawn for thee;
        But then my mother's sleep is light,
        Were we surprised by her, ah me!
        Upon the spot I should be dead.
FAUST.   Dear angel! there's no cause for dread.
        Here is a little phial, — if she take
        Mixed in her drink three drops, 'twill steep
        Her nature in a deep and soothing sleep.
MARG.   What do I not for thy dear sake!
        To her it will not harmful prove?
FAUST.   Should I advise it else, sweet love?
MARG.   I know not, dearest, when thy face I see,
        What doth my spirit to thy will constrain;
        Already I have done so much for thee,
        That scarcely more to do doth now remain.   [Exit.]

MEPHISTOPHELES enters.

MEPH.   The monkey! Is she gone?
FAUST.   Again hast played the spy?
MEPH.   Of all that pass'd I'm well apprized,
        I heard the doctor catechised,
        And trust he'll profit much thereby!
        Fain would the girls inquire indeed
        Touching their lover's faith and creed,
        And whether pious in the good old way;
        They think, if pliant there, us too he will obey.

FAUST.   Thou monster, does not see that this
  Pure soul, possessed by ardent love,
  Full of the living faith,
  To her of bliss
  The only pledge, must holy anguish prove,
  Holding the man she loves, fore-doomed to endless death!
MEPH.   Most sensual, supersensualist? The while
  A damsel leads thee by the nose!
FAUST.   Of filth and fire abortion vile!
MEPH.   In physiognomy strange skill she shows;
  She in my presence feels she knows not how;
  My mask it seems a hidden sense reveals;
  That I'm a genius she must needs allow,
  That I'm the very devil perhaps she feels.
  So then to-night—
FAUST.   What's that to you?
MEPH.   I've my amusement in it too!

SCENE—*At the Well*

MARGARET *and* BESSY, *with pitchers.*

BESSY.   Of Barbara hast nothing heard?
MARG.   I rarely go from home,—no, not a word.
BESSY.   'Tis true: Sybilla told me so to-day!
  That comes of being proud, methinks;
  She played the fool at last.
MARG.   How so?
BESSY.   They say
  That two she feedeth when she eats and drinks.
MARG.   Alas!
BESSY.   She's rightly served, in sooth,
  How long she hung upon the youth!
  What promenades, what jaunts there were,
  To dancing booth and village fair!
  The first she everywhere must shine,
  He always treating her to pastry and to wine
  Of her good looks she was so vain,
  So shameless too, that to retain

His presents, she did not disdain;
Sweet words and kisses came anon —
And then the virgin flower was gone.

MARG.   Poor thing!
BESSY.   Forsooth dost pity her?
At night, when at our wheels we sat,
Abroad our mothers ne'er would let us stir.
Then with her lover she must chat,
Or on the bench or in the dusky walk,
Thinking the hours too brief for their sweet talk;
Her proud head she will have to bow,
And in white sheet do penance now!

MARG.   But he will surely marry her?
BESSY.   Not he!
He won't be such a fool! a gallant lad
Like him, can roam o'er land and sea,
Besides, he's off.

MARG.   That is not fair!
BESSY.   If she should get him, 'twere almost as bad!
Her myrtle wreath the boys would tear;
And then we girls would plague her too,
For we chopp'd straw before her door would strew!   [*Exit.*]

MARG.   [*Walking towards home*] How stoutly once I could inveigh,
If a poor maiden went astray;
Not words enough my tongue could find,
'Gainst others' sin to speak my mind!
Black as it seemed, I blacken'd it still more,
And strove to make it blacker than before.
And did myself securely bless —
Now my own trespass doth appear!
Yet ah! — what urg'd me to transgress,
God knows, it was so sweet, so dear!

SCENE — *Zwinger*

Enclosure between the City-wall and the Gate. In the niche of the wall a
devotional image of the Mater dolorosa, with flower-pots before it.

MARG.   [*Putting fresh flowers in the pots*] Ah, rich in sorrow, thou,
Stoop thy maternal brow,
And mark with pitying eye my misery!
The sword in thy pierced heart,
Thou dost with bitter smart,
Gaze upwards on thy Son's death agony.
To the dear God on high,
Ascends thy piteous sigh,
Pleading for his and thy sore misery.
Ah, who can know
The torturing woe,
The pangs that rack me to the bone?
How my poor heart, without relief,
Trembles and throbs, its yearning grief
Thou knowest, thou alone!
Ah, wheresoe'er I go,
With woe, with woe, with woe,
My anguish'd breast is aching!
When all alone I creep,
I weep, I weep, I weep,
Alas! my heart is breaking!
The flower-pots at my window
Were wet with tears of mine,
The while I pluck'd these blossoms,
At dawn to deck thy shrine!
When early in my chamber
Shone bright the rising morn,
I sat there on my pallet,
My heart with anguish torn.
Help! from disgrace and death deliver me!
Ah! rich in sorrow, thou,
Stoop thy maternal brow,
And mark with pitying eye my misery!

SCENE—*Night—Street Before* MARGARET'S *Door*

VALENTINE (*a soldier,* MARGARET'S *brother*).

VAL.   When seated 'mong the jovial crowd,
        Where merry comrades boasting loud
        Each named with pride his favourite lass,
        And in her honour drain'd his glass;
        Upon my elbows I would lean,
        With easy quiet view the scene,
        Nor give my tongue the rein until
        Each swaggering blade had talked his fill.
        Then smiling I my beard would stroke,
        The while, with brimming glass, I spoke;
        "Each to his taste—but to my mind,
        Where in the country will you find
        A maid, as my dear Gretchen fair,
        Who with my sister can compare?"
        Cling! Clang! so rang the jovial sound!
        Shouts of assent went circling round;
        Pride of her sex is she!—cried some;
        Then were the noisy boasters dumb.

        And now!—I could tear out my hair,
        Or dash my brains out in despair!—
        Me every scurvy knave may twit,
        With stinging jest and taunting sneer!
        Like skulking debtor I must sit,
        And sweat each casual word to hear!
        And though I smash'd them one and all,—
        Yet them I could not liars call.

            Who comes this way? who's sneaking here?
            If I mistake not, two draw near.
            If he be one, have at him;—well I wot
            Alive he shall not leave this spot!

FAUST, MEPHISTOPHELES.

FAUST.   How from yon sacristy, athwart the night,
         Its beams the ever-burning taper throws,
         While ever waning, fades the glimmering light,

As gathering darkness doth around it close!
So night-like gloom doth in my bosom reign.
MEPH.   I'm like a tom-cat in a thievish vein,
That up fire-ladders tall and steep,
And round the walls doth slyly creep;
Virtuous withal, I feel, with, I confess,
A touch of thievish joy and wantonness.
Thus through my limbs already burns
The glorious Walpurgis night!
After to-morrow it returns,
Then why one wakes, one knows aright!
FAUST.   Meanwhile, the treasure I see glimmering there,
Will it ascend into the open air?
MEPH.   Ere long thou wilt proceed with pleasure,
To raise the casket with its treasure;
I took a peep, therein are stored,
Of lion-dollars a rich hoard.
FAUST.   And not a trinket? not a ring?
Wherewith my lovely girl to deck?
MEPH.   I saw among them some such thing,
A string of pearls to grace her neck.
FAUST.   'Tis well! I'm always loath to go,
Without some gift my love to show.
MEPH.   Some pleasures gratis to enjoy,
Should surely cause you no annoy.
While bright with stars the heavens appear,
I'll sing a masterpiece of art:
A moral song shall charm her ear,
More surely to beguile her heart.

[*Sings to the guitar*]

Kathrina say,
Why lingering stay
At dawn of day
Before your lover's door?
Maiden, beware,
Nor enter there,
Lest forth you fare,
A maiden never more.

Maiden take heed!
Reck well my rede![1]
Is't done, the deed?
Good night, you poor, poor thing!
The spoiler's lies,
His arts despise,
Nor yield your prize,
Without the marriage ring!

VAL.   [*Steps forward*]. Whom are you luring here? I'll give it you!
Accursed rat-catchers, your strains I'll end!
First, to the devil the guitar I'll send!
Then to the devil with the singer too!

MEPH.   The poor guitar! 'tis done for now.

VAL.   Your skull shall follow next, I trow!

MEPH.   [*To* FAUST] Doctor, stand fast! your strength collect!
Be prompt, and do as I direct.
Out with your whisk, keep close, I pray,
I'll parry! do you thrust away!

VAL.   Then parry that!

MEPH.   Why not?

VAL.   That too!

MEPH.   With ease!

VAL.   The devil fights for you!
Why how is this? my hand's already lamed!

MEPH.   [*To* FAUST] Thrust home!

VAL.   [*Falls*] Alas!

MEPH.   There! Now the lubber's tamed!
But quick, away! We must at once take wing;
A cry of murder strikes upon the ear;
With the police I know my course to steer,
But with the blood-ban 'tis another thing.

MARTHA.   [*At the window*] Without! without!

MARG.   [*At the window*] Quick, bring a light!

MARTHA.   [*As above*] They rail and scuffle, scream and fight!

PEOPLE.   One lieth here already dead!

MARTHA.   [*Coming out*] Where are the murderers? are they fled?

MARG.   [*Coming out*] Who lieth here?

---

1. *rede*] story, account or advice.

PEOPLE.   Thy mother's son.

MARG.   Almighty God! I am undone!

VAL.   I'm dying — 'tis a soon-told tale,
    And sooner done the deed.
    Why, women, do ye howl and wail?
    To my last words give heed!   [*All gather round him.*]
    My Gretchen, see! still young art thou,
    Art not discreet enough, I trow,
    Thou dost thy matters ill;
    Let this in confidence be said:
    Since thou the path of shame dost tread,
    Tread it with right good will!

MARG.   My brother! God! what can this mean?

VAL.   Abstain,
    Nor dare God's holy name profane!
    What's done, alas, is done and past!
    Matters will take their course at last;
    By stealth thou dost begin with one,
    Others will follow him anon;
    And when a dozen thee have known,
    Thou'lt common be to all the town.
    When infamy is newly born,
    In secret she is brought to light,
    And the mysterious veil of night
    O'er head and ears is drawn;
    The loathsome birth men fain would slay;
    But soon, full grown, she waxes bold,
    And though not fairer to behold,
    With brazen front insults the day:
    The more abhorrent to the sight,
    The more she courts the day's pure light.

    The time already I discern,
    When thee all honest folk will spurn,
    And shun thy hated form to meet,
    As when a corpse infects the street.
    Thy heart will sink in blank despair,
    When they shall look thee in the face!
    A golden chain no more thou'lt wear!
    Nor near the altar take in church thy place!

In fair lace collar simply dight
Thou'lt dance no more with spirits light!
In darksome corners thou wilt bide,
Where beggars vile and cripples hide,
And e'en though God thy crime forgive,
On earth, a thing accursed, thou'lt live!

MARTHA.   Your parting soul to God commend!
Your dying breath in slander will spend?

VAL.   Could I but reach thy wither'd frame,
Thou wretched beldame, void of shame!
Full measure I might hope to win
Of pardon then for every sin.

MARG.   Brother! what agonizing pain!

VAL.   I tell thee, from vain tears abstain!
'Twas thy dishonour pierced my heart,
Thy fall the fatal death-stab gave.
Through the death-sleep I now depart
To God, a soldier true and brave.   [*Dies.*]

SCENE — *Cathedral — Service, Organ, and Anthem*

MARGARET *amongst a number of people.* EVIL-SPIRIT *behind* MARGARET.

EVIL-SPIRIT.   How different, Gretchen, was it once with thee,
When thou, still full of innocence,
Here to the altar camest,
And from the small and well-conn'd book
Didst lisp thy prayer,
Half childish sport,
Half God in thy young heart!
Gretchen!
What thoughts are thine?
What deed of shame
Lurks in thy sinful heart?
Is thy prayer utter'd for thy mother's soul,
Who into long, long torment slept through thee?
Whose blood is on thy threshold?

> —And stirs there not already 'neath thy heart
> Another quick'ning pulse, that even now
> Tortures itself and thee
> With its foreboding presence?

MARG.   Woe! Woe!
> Oh could I free me from the thoughts
> That hither, thither, crowd upon my brain,
> Against my will!

CHORUS

> *Dies iræ, dies illa,*
> *Solvet sæclum in favilla.*[1]

> [*The organ sounds.*]

EVIL-SPIRIT.   Grim horror seizes thee!
> The trumpet sounds!
> The graves are shaken!
> And thy heart
> From ashy rest
> For torturing flames
> Anew created,
> Trembles into life!

MARG.   Would I were hence!
> It is as if the organ
> Choked my breath,
> As if the choir
> Melted my inmost heart!

CHORUS

> *Judex ergo cum sedebit,*
> *Quidquid latet apparebit,*
> *Nil inultum remanebit.*[2]

MARG.   I feel oppressed!
> The pillars of the wall
> Imprison me!
> The vaulted roof
> Weighs down upon me! —air!

EVIL-SPIRIT.   Wouldst hide thee? sin and shame

---

1. *Dies . . . favilla*] "The day of wrath, that day, will dissolve the world in flames." This and the following lines in Latin are taken from the requiem mass.
2. *Judex . . . remanebit*] "Thus when the judge will sit, all that is hidden will appear, nothing will remain unpunished."

Remain not hidden!
Air! light!
Woe's thee!

CHORUS

Quid sum miser tunc dicturus?
Quem patronum rogaturus!
Cum vix justus sit securus.[3]

EVIL-SPIRIT.   The glorified their faces turn
Away from thee!
Shudder the pure to reach
Their hands to thee!
Woe!

CHORUS

Quid sum miser tunc dicturus —

MARG.   Neighbour! your smelling bottle!   [*She swoons away.*]

SCENE — *Walpurgis-Night — The Harz Mountains.*
District of Schierke and Elend.

FAUST *and* MEPHISTOPHELES.

MEPH.   A broomstick dost thou not at least desire?
The roughest he-goat fain would I bestride,
By this road from our goal we're still far wide.
FAUST.   While fresh upon my legs, so long I naught require,
Except this knotty staff. Beside,
What boots it to abridge a pleasant way?
Along the labyrinth of these vales to creep,
Then scale these rocks, whence, in eternal spray,
Adown the cliffs the silvery fountains leap:
Such is the joy that seasons paths like these!
Spring weaves already in the birchen trees;
E'en the late pine-grove feels her quickening powers;
Should she not work within these limbs of ours?
MEPH.   Naught of this genial influence do I know!
Within me all is wintry. Frost and snow

3. *Quid . . . securus*] "What shall I then say in my wretchedness, what protector shall I call upon, when even the just man is barely safe?"

I should prefer my dismal path to bound.
How sadly, yonder, with belated glow
Rises the ruddy moon's imperfect round,
Shedding so faint a light, at every tread
One's sure to stumble 'gainst a rock or tree!
An Ignis Fatuus[1] I must call instead.
Yonder one burning merrily, I see.
Holla! my friend! may I request your light?
Why should you flare away so uselessly?
Be kind enough to show us up the height!

IGNIS FATUUS.   Through reverence, I hope I may subdue
    The lightness of my nature; true,
    Our course is but a zigzag one.

MEPH.   Ho! ho!
    So men, forsooth, he thinks to imitate!
    Now, in the devil's name, for once go straight!
    Or out at once your flickering life I'll blow.

IGNIS FATUUS.   That you are master here is obvious quite;
    To do your will, I'll cordially essay;
    Only reflect! The hill is magic-mad to-night;
    And if to show the path you choose a meteor's light,
    You must not wonder should we go astray.

FAUST, MEPH.,   ⎫
IGNIS FATUUS.   ⎬   [*In alternate song*]
             ⎭

        Through the dream and magic-sphere,
        As it seems, we now are speeding;
        Honour win, us rightly leading,
        That betimes we may appear
        In yon wide and desert region!

        Trees on trees, a stalwart legion,
        Swiftly past us are retreating,
        And the cliffs with lowly greeting;
        Rocks long-snouted, row on row,
        How they snort, and how they blow!

        Through the stones and heather springing,
        Brook and brooklet haste below;
        Hark the rustling! Hark the singing!
        Hearken to love's plaintive lays;

---

1. *Ignis Fatuus*] will-o'-the-wisp; literally, foolish fire; a deceptive goal or hope.

Voices of those heavenly days —
What we hope, and what we love!
Like a tale of olden time,
Echo's voice prolongs the chime.

To-whit! To-whoo! It sounds more near;
Plover, owl and jay appear,
All awake, around, above?
Paunchy salamanders too
Peer, long-limbed, the bushes through!
And, like snakes, the roots of trees
Coil themselves from rock and sand,
Stretching many a wondrous band,
Us to frighten, us to seize;
From rude knots with life embued,
Polyp-fangs abroad they spread,
To snare the wanderer! 'Neath our tread,
Mice, in myriads, thousand-hued,
Through the heath and through the moss!
And the fire-flies' glittering throng,
Wildering escort, whirls along,
Here and there, our path across.
Tell me, stand we motionless,
Or still forward do we press?
All things round us whirl and fly;
Rocks and trees make strange grimaces,
Dazzling meteors change their places,
How they puff and multiply!

MEPH.   Now grasp my doublet — we at last
A central peak have reached, which shows,
If round a wondering glance we cast,
How in the mountain Mammon[2] glows.
FAUST.   How through the chasms strangely gleams,
A lurid light, like dawn's red glow,
Pervading with its quivering beams,
The gorges of the gulf below!
Here vapours rise, there clouds float by,
Here through the mist the light doth shine;
Now, like a fount, it bursts on high,

2. *Mammon*] in the New Testament, riches; as a proper name, the demon of cupidity.

Meanders now, a slender line;
Far reaching, with a hundred veins,
Here through the valley see it glide;
Here, where its force the gorge restrains,
At once it scatters, far and wide;
Anear, like showers of golden sand
Strewn broadcast, sputter sparks of light:
And mark yon rocky walls that stand
Ablaze, in all their towering height!

MEPH.   Doth not Sir Mammon for this fête
Grandly illume his palace! Thou
Art lucky to have seen it; now,
The boisterous guests, I feel, are coming straight.

FAUST.   How through the air the storm doth whirl!
Upon my neck it strikes with sudden shock.

MEPH.   Cling to these ancient ribs of granite rock,
Else to yon depths profound it you will hurl.
A murky vapour thickens night.
Hark! Through the woods the tempests roar!
The owlets flit in wild affright.
Hark! Splinter'd are the columns that upbore
The leafy palace, green for aye:
The shivered branches whirr and sigh,
Yawn the huge trunks with mighty groan.
The roots upriven, creak and moan!
In fearful and entangled fall,
One crashing ruin whelms them all,
While through the desolate abyss,
Sweeping the wreck-strewn precipice,
The raging storm-blasts howl and hiss!
Aloft strange voices dost thou hear?
Distant now and now more near?
Hark! the mountain ridge along,
Streameth a raving magic-song!

WITCHES.   [*In chorus*] Now to the Brocken[3] the witches hie,
The stubble is yellow, the corn is green;
Thither the gathering legions fly,
And sitting aloft is Sir Urian seen:

3. *Brocken*] highest mountain in the Harz range.

O'er stick and o'er stone they go whirling along,
Witches and he-goats, a motley throng.
VOICES.   Alone old Baubo's[4] coming now;
She rides upon a farrow sow.

CHORUS

Honour to her, to whom honour is due!
Forward, Dame Baubo! Honour to you!
A goodly sow and mother thereon,
The whole witch chorus follows anon.

VOICE.   Which way didst come?
VOICE.   O'er Ilsenstein!
There I peep'd in an owlet's nest.
With her broad eye she gazed in mine!
VOICE.   Drive to the devil, thou hellish pest!
Why ride so hard?
VOICE.   She has graz'd my side,
Look at the wounds, how deep and how wide!
WITCHES.   [*In chorus*] The way is broad, the way is long;
What mad pursuit! What tumult wild!
Scratches the besom[5] and sticks the prong;
Crush'd is the mother, and stifled the child.
WIZARDS.   [*Half chorus*] Like house-encumber'd snail we creep;
While far ahead the women keep,
For when to the devil's house we speed,
By a thousand steps they take the lead.
THE OTHER HALF.   Not so, precisely do we view it; —
They with a thousand steps may do it;
But let them hasten as they can,
With one long bound 'tis clear'd by man.
VOICES.   [*Above*] Come with us, come with us from Felsensee.
VOICES.   [*From below*] Aloft to you we would mount with glee!
We wash, and free from all stain are we,
Yet barren evermore must be!

BOTH CHORUSES

The wind is hushed, the stars grow pale,
The pensive moon her light doth veil;

4. *Baubo*] Greek goddess of a phallic cult; in *Faust, Part Two*, she symbolizes sensuality.
5. *besom*] broom made of twigs.

> And whirling on, the magic choir
> Sputters forth sparks of drizzling fire.

VOICE.   [*From below*] Stay! stay!
VOICE.   [*From above*]   What voice of woe
> Calls from the cavern'd depths below?

VOICE.   [*From below*] Take me with you! Oh take me too!
> Three centuries I climb in vain,
> And yet can ne'er the summit gain!
> To be with my kindred I am fain.

BOTH CHORUSES

> Broom and pitch-fork, goat and prong,
> Mounted on these we whirl along;
> Who vainly strives to climb to-night,
> Is evermore a luckless wight![6]

DEMI-WITCH.   [*Below*] I hobble after, many a day;
> Already the others are far away!
> No rest at home can I obtain —
> Here too my efforts are in vain!

CHORUS OF WITCHES

> Salve gives the witches strength to rise;
> A rag for a sail does well enough;
> A goodly ship is every trough;
> To-night who flies not, never flies.

BOTH CHORUSES

> And when the topmost peak we round,
> Then alight ye on the ground;
> The heath's wide regions cover ye
> With your mad swarms of witchery!

> > > [*They let themselves down.*]

MEPH.   They crowd and jostle, whirl and flutter!
> They whisper, babble, twirl, and splutter!
> They glimmer, sparkle, stink and flare —
> A true witch-element! Beware!
> Stick close! else we shall severed be.
> Where art thou?

FAUST.   [*In the distance*] Here!
MEPH.   Already, whirl'd so far away!

---

6. *wight*] creature, living being, esp. a human being.

The master then indeed I needs must play.
Give ground! Squire Voland[7] comes! Sweet folk, give ground!
Here, doctor, grasp me! With a single bound
Let us escape this ceaseless jar;
Even for me too mad these people are.
Hard by there shineth something with peculiar glare,
Yon brake allureth me; it is not far;
Come, come along with me! we'll slip in there.

FAUST.   Spirit of contradiction! Lead! I'll follow straight!
'Twas wisely done, however, to repair
On May-night to the Brocken, and when there
By our own choice ourselves to isolate!

MEPH.   Mark, of those flames the motley glare!
A merry club assembles there.
In a small circle one is not alone.

FAUST.   I'd rather be above, though, I must own!
Already fire and eddying smoke I view;
The impetuous millions to the devil ride;
Full many a riddle will be there untied.

MEPH.   Ay! and full many a riddle tied anew.
But let the great world rave and riot!
Here will we house ourselves in quiet.
A custom 'tis of ancient date,
Our lesser worlds within the great world to create!
Young witches there I see, naked and bare,
And old ones, veil'd more prudently.
For my sake only courteous be!
The trouble's small, the sport is rare.
Of instruments I hear the cursed din —
One must get used to it. Come in! come in!
There's now no help for it. I'll step before
And introducing you as my good friend,
Confer on you one obligation more.
How say you now? 'Tis no such paltry room;
Why only look, you scarce can see the end.
A hundred fires in rows disperse the gloom;
They dance, they talk, they cook, make love, and drink:
Where could we find aught better, do you think?

FAUST.   To introduce us, do you purpose here

7. *Voland*] German for evil fiend.

As devil or as wizard to appear?
MEPH.   Though I am wont indeed to strict incognito,
          Yet upon gala-days one must one's orders show.
          No garter have I to distinguish me,
          Nathless the cloven foot doth here give dignity.
          Seest thou yonder snail? Crawling this way she hies:
          With searching feelers, she, no doubt,
          Hath me already scented out;
          Here, even if I would, for me there's no disguise.
          From fire to fire, we'll saunter at our leisure,
          The gallant you, I'll cater for your pleasure.

                    [*To a party seated round some expiring embers.*]

Old gentleman, apart, why sit ye moping here?
Ye in the midst should be of all this jovial cheer,
Girt round with noise and youthful riot;
At home one surely has enough of quiet.
GENERAL.   In nations put his trust, who may,
          Whate'er for them one may have done;
          For with the people, as with women, they
          Honour your rising stars alone!
MINISTER.   Now all too far they wander from the right;
          I praise the good old ways, to them I hold,
          Then was the genuine age of gold,
          When we ourselves were foremost in men's sight.
PARVENU.   Ne'er were we 'mong your dullards found,
          And what we ought not, that to do were fair;
          Yet now are all things turning round and round,
          When on firm basis we would them maintain.
AUTHOR.   Who, as a rule, a treatise now would care
          To read, of even moderate sense?
          As for the rising generation, ne'er
          Has youth displayed such arrogant pretence.
MEPH.   [*Suddenly appearing very old*] Since for the last time I the
              Brocken scale,
          That folk are ripe for doomsday, now one sees;
          And just because my cask begins to fail,
          So the whole world is also on the lees.
HUCKSTER-WITCH.   Stop, gentlemen, nor pass me by,
          Of wares I have a choice collection:
          Pray honour them with your inspection.

Lose not this opportunity!
Yet nothing in my booth you'll find
Without its counterpart on earth; there's naught,
Which to the world, and to mankind,
Hath not some direful mischief wrought.
No dagger here, which hath not flow'd with blood,
No chalice, whence, into some healthy frame
Hath not been poured hot poison's wasting flood.
No trinket, but hath wrought some woman's shame,
No weapon but hath cut some sacred tie,
Or from behind hath stabb'd an enemy.

MEPH.   Gossip! For wares like these the time's gone by,
What's done is past! what's past is done!
With novelties your booth supply;
Us novelties attract alone.

FAUST.   May this wild scene my senses spare!
This, may in truth be called a fair!

MEPH.   Upward the eddying concourse throng;
Thinking to push, thyself art push'd along.

FAUST.   Who's that, pray?

MEPH.   Mark her well! That's Lilith.

FAUST.   Who?

MEPH.   Adam's first wife. Of her rich locks beware!
That charm in which she's parallel'd by few;
When in its toils a youth she doth ensnare,
He will not soon escape, I promise you.

FAUST.   There sit a pair, the old one with the young;
Already they have bravely danced and sprung!

MEPH.   Here there is no repose to-day.
Another dance begins; we'll join it, come away!

FAUST.   [*Dancing with the young one*] Once a fair vision came to me;
Therein I saw an apple-tree,
Two beauteous apples charmed mine eyes;
I climb'd forthwith to reach the prize.

THE FAIR ONE.   Apples still fondly ye desire,
From paradise it hath been so.
Feelings of joy my breast inspire
That such too in my garden grow.

MEPH.   [*With the old one*] Once a weird vision came to me;
Therein I saw a rifted tree.
It had a . . . . . . ;

But as it was it pleased me too.

THE OLD ONE.   I beg most humbly to salute
The gallant with the cloven foot!
Let him a . . . have ready here,
If he a . . . does not fear.

PROCTOPHANTASMIST.   Accursed mob! How dare ye thus to meet?
Have I not shown and demonstrated too,
That ghosts stand not on ordinary feet?
Yet here ye dance, as other mortals do!

THE FAIR ONE.   [*Dancing*] Then at our ball, what doth he here?

FAUST.   [*Dancing*] Oh! He must everywhere appear.
He must adjudge, when others dance;
If on each step his say's not said,
So is that step as good as never made.
He's most annoyed, so soon as we advance;
If ye would circle in one narrow round,
As he in his old mill, then doubtless he
Your dancing would approve, — especially
If ye forthwith salute him with respect profound!

PROCTOPHANTASMIST.   Still here! what arrogance! unheard of quite!
Vanish; we now have fill'd the world with light!
Laws are unheeded by the devil's host;
Wise as we are, yet Tegel[8] hath its ghost!
How long at this conceit I've swept with all my might,
Lost is the labour: 'tis unheard of quite!

THE FAIR ONE.   Cease here to teaze us any more, I pray.

PROCTOPHANTASMIST.   Spirits, I plainly to your face declare:
No spiritual control myself will bear,
Since my own spirit can exert no sway.

[*The dancing continues.*]

To-night, I see, I shall in naught succeed;
But I'm prepar'd my travels to pursue,
And hope, before my final step indeed,
To triumph over bards and devils too.

MEPH.   Now in some puddle will he take his station,
Such is his mode of seeking consolation;
Where leeches, feasting on his rump, will drain

8. *Tegel*] A locality near Berlin, where the Enlightenment writer and bookseller Christoph Friedrich Nicolai (whom Goethe pillories as the Proctophantasmist) reported a haunting.

Spirits alike and spirit from his brain.
[*To* FAUST, *who has left the dance*] But why the charming damsel
leave, I pray,
Who to you in the dance so sweetly sang?

FAUST.   Ah, in the very middle of her lay,
Out of her mouth a small red mouse there sprang.

MEPH.   Suppose there did! One must not be too nice.
'Twas well it was not grey, let that suffice.
Who 'mid his pleasures for a trifle cares?

FAUST.   Then saw I —

MEPH.   What?

FAUST.   Mephisto, seest thou there
Standing far off, a lone child, pale and fair?
Slow from the spot her drooping form she tears,
And seems with shackled feet to move along;
I own, within me the delusion's strong,
That she the likeness of my Gretchen wears.

MEPH.   Gaze not upon her! 'Tis not good! Forbear!
'Tis lifeless, magical, a shape of air,
An idol. Such to meet with, bodes no good;
That rigid look of hers doth freeze man's blood,
And well-nigh petrifies his heart to stone: —
The story of Medusa[9] thou hast known.

FAUST.   Ay, verily! a corpse's eyes are those,
Which there was no fond loving hand to close.
That is the bosom I so fondly press'd,
That my sweet Gretchen's form, so oft caress'd!

MEPH.   Deluded fool! 'Tis magic, I declare!
To each she doth his lov'd one's image wear.

FAUST.   What bliss! what torture! vainly I essay
To turn me from that piteous look away.
How strangely doth a single crimson line
Around that lovely neck its coil entwine,
It shows no broader than a knife's blunt edge!

MEPH.   Quite right. I see it also, and allege
That she beneath her arm her head can bear,
Since Perseus cut it off. — But you I swear

---

9. *Medusa*] in Greek mythology, one of three snake-haired sisters whose glance could turn
the beholder into stone.

Are craving for illusion still!
Come then, ascend yon little hill!
As on the Prater all is gay,
And if my senses are not gone,
I see a theatre, — what's going on?

SERVIBILIS.   They are about to recommence; — the play
Will be the last of seven, and spick-span new —
'Tis usual here that number to present.
A dilettante did the piece invent,
And dilettanti will enact it too.
Excuse me, gentlemen; to me's assign'd
As dilettante to uplift the curtain.

MEPH.   You on the Blocksberg I'm rejoiced to find,
That 'tis your most appropriate sphere is certain.

SCENE — *Walpurgis-Night's Dream, or Oberon and Titania's*
Golden Wedding-feast — Theatre

Intermezzo

MANAGER.   Vales, where mists still shift and play,
                     To ancient hills succeeding, —
                 These our scenes; — so we, to-day,
                     May rest, brave sons of Mieding.[1]

HERALD.   That the marriage golden be,
                     Must fifty years be ended;
                 More dear this feast of gold to me,
                     Contention now suspended.

OBERON.   Spirits, if present, grace the scene,
                     And if with me united,
                 Then gratulate the king and queen,
                     Their troth thus newly plighted!

PUCK.   Puck draws near and wheels about,
                     In mazy circles dancing!
                 Hundreds swell his joyous shout,
                     Behind him still advancing.

---

1. *sons of Mieding*] theatrical technicians; Mieding was the chief carpenter at Goethe's
court theatre in Weimar.

ARIEL.	Ariel wakes his dainty air,
	His lyre celestial stringing. —
	Fools he lureth, and the fair,
	With his celestial singing.
OBERON.	Wedded ones, would ye agree,
	We court your imitation:
	Would ye fondly love as we,
	We counsel separation.
TITANIA.	If husband scold and wife retort,
	Then bear them far asunder;
	Her to the burning south transport,
	And him the North Pole under.

THE WHOLE ORCHESTRA.   [*Fortissimo*] Flies and midges all unite
        With frog and chirping cricket,
        One orchestra throughout the night,
        Resounding in the thicket!

[*Solo*]

        Yonder doth the bagpipe come!
        Its sack an airy bubble.
        Schnick, schnick, schnack, with nasal hum,
        Its notes it doth redouble.

EMBRYO SPIRIT.   Spider's foot and midge's wing,
        A toad in form and feature;
        Together verses it can string,
        Though scarce a living creature.

A LITTLE PAIR.   Tiny step and lofty bound,
        Through dew and exhalation;
        Ye trip it deftly on the ground,
        But gain no elevation.

INQUISITIVE TRAVELLER.   Can I indeed believe my eyes?
        Is't not mere masquerading?
        What! Oberon in beauteous guise,
        Among the groups parading!

ORTHODOX.   No claws, no tail to whisk about,
        To fright us at our revel; —
        Yet like the gods of Greece, no doubt,
        He too's a genuine devil.

NORTHERN ARTIST.   These that I'm hitting off to-day
        Are sketches unpretending;
        Towards Italy without delay,

                    My steps I think of bending.
PURIST.   Alas! ill-fortune leads me here,
                    Where riot still grows louder;
                And 'mong the witches gather'd here
                    But two alone wear powder!
YOUNG WITCH.   Your powder and your petticoat,
                    Suit hags, there's no gainsaying;
                Hence I sit fearless on my goat,
                    My naked charms displaying.
MATRON.   We're too well-bred to squabble here,
                    Or insult back to render;
                But may you wither soon, my dear,
                    Although so young and tender.
LEADER OF THE BAND.   Nose of fly and gnat's proboscis,
                    Throng not the naked beauty!
                Frogs and crickets in the mosses,
                    Keep time and do your duty!
WEATHERCOCK.   [*Towards one side*] What charming company I view
                    Together here collected!
                Gay bachelors, a hopeful crew,
                    And brides so unaffected!
WEATHERCOCK.   [*Towards the other side*] Unless indeed the yawning
    ground
                    Should open to receive them.
                From this vile crew, with sudden bound,
                    To Hell I'd jump and leave them,
XENIEN.   With small sharp shears, in insect guise
                    Behold us at your revel!
                That we may tender, filial-wise,
                    Our homage to the devil.
HENNINGS.   Look now at yonder eager crew,
                    How naïvely they're jesting!
                That they have tender hearts and true,
                    They stoutly keep protesting!
MUSAGET.   Oneself amid this witchery
                    How pleasantly one loses;
                For witches easier are to me
                    To govern than the Muses!
CI-DEVANT GENIUS OF THE AGE.   With proper folks when we appear,
                    No one can then surpass us!
                Keep close, wide is the Blocksberg here

As Germany's Parnassus.

INQUISITIVE TRAVELLER.   How name ye that stiff formal man,
Who strides with lofty paces?
He tracks the game where'er he can,
"He scents the Jesuits' traces."

CRANE.   Where waters troubled are or clear,
To fish I am delighted;
Thus pious gentlemen appear
With devils here united.

WORLDLING. By pious people, it is true,
No medium is rejected;
Conventicles, and not a few,
On Blocksberg are erected.

DANCER.   Another chorus now succeeds,
Far off the drums are beating.
Be still! The bitterns 'mong the reeds
Their one note are repeating.

DANCING MASTER.   Each twirls about and never stops,
And as he can he fareth.
The crooked leaps, the clumsy hops,
Nor for appearance careth.

FIDDLER.   To take each other's life, I trow,
Would cordially delight them!
As Orpheus' lyre the beasts, so now
The bagpipe doth unite them.

DOGMATIST. My views, in spite of doubt and sneer,
I hold with stout persistence,
Inferring from the devils here,
The evil one's existence.

IDEALIST.   My every sense rules Phantasy
With sway quite too potential;
Sure I'm demented if the *I*
Alone is the essential.

REALIST.   This entity's a dreadful bore,
And cannot choose but vex me;
The ground beneath me ne'er before
Thus totter'd to perplex me.

SUPERNATURALIST.   Well pleased assembled here I view
Of spirits this profusion;
From devils, touching angels too,
I gather some conclusion.

SCEPTIC. The ignis fatuus they track out,
And think they're near the treasure.
Devil alliterates with doubt,
Here I abide with pleasure.

LEADER OF THE BAND. Frog and cricket in the mosses, —
Confound your gasconading!
Nose of fly and gnat's proboscis; —
Most tuneful serenading!

THE KNOWING ONES. Sans-souci, so this host we greet,
Their jovial humour showing;
There's now no walking on our feet,
So on our heads we're going.

THE AWKWARD ONES. In seasons past we snatch'd, 'tis true,
Some tit-bits by our cunning;
Our shoes, alas, are now danced through,
On our bare soles we're running.

WILL-O'-THE-WISPS. From marshy bogs we sprang to light,
Yet here behold us dancing;
The gayest gallants of the night,
In glitt'ring rows advancing.

SHOOTING STAR. With rapid motion from on high,
I shot in starry splendour;
Now prostrate on the grass I lie; —
Who aid will kindly render?

THE MASSIVE ONES. Room! wheel round! They're coming, lo!
Down sink the bending grasses.
Though spirits, yet their limbs, we know,
Are huge substantial masses.

PUCK. Don't stamp so heavily, I pray;
Like elephants you're treading!
And 'mong the elves be Puck to-day,
The stoutest at the wedding!

ARIEL. If nature boon, or subtle sprite,
Endow your soul with pinions; —
Then follow to yon rosy height,
Through ether's calm dominions!

ORCHESTRA. [*Pianissimo*] Drifting cloud and misty wreathes
Are fill'd with light elysian;
O'er reed and leaf the zephyr breathes —
So fades the fairy vision!

SCENE—*A Gloomy Day—A Plain*

FAUST *and* MEPHISTOPHELES.

FAUST. In misery! despairing! long wandering pitifully on the face of
the earth and now imprisoned! This gentle hapless creature, im-
mured in the dungeon as a malefactor and reserved for horrid tor-
tures! That it should come to this! To this!—Perfidious, worthless
spirit, and this thou hast concealed from me!—Stand! ay, stand! roll
in malicious rage thy fiendish eyes! Stand and brave me with thine
insupportable presence! Imprisoned! In hopeless misery! Delivered
over to the power of evil spirits and the judgment of unpitying
humanity!—And me, the while, thou wert lulling with tasteless dis-
sipations, concealing from me her growing anguish, and leaving her
to perish without help!

MEPH. She is not the first.

FAUST. Hound! Execrable monster!—Back with him, oh thou infinite
spirit! back with the reptile into his dog's shape, in which it was his
wont to scamper before me at eventide, to roll before the feet of the
harmless wanderer, and to fasten on his shoulders when he fell!
Change him again into his favourite shape, that he may crouch on his
belly before me in the dust, whilst I spurn him with my foot, the
reprobate!—Not the first!—Woe! Woe! By no human soul is it con-
ceivable, that more than one human creature has ever sunk into a
depth of wretchedness like this, or that the first in her writhing death-
agony should not have atoned in the sight of all-pardoning Heaven for
the guilt of all the rest! The misery of this one pierces me to the very
marrow, and harrows up my soul; thou art grinning calmly over the
doom of thousands!

MEPH. Now we are once again at our wit's end, just where the reason
of you mortals snaps! Why dost thou seek our fellowship, if thou canst
not go through with it? Wilt fly, and art not proof against dizziness?
Did we force ourselves on thee, or thou on us?

FAUST. Cease thus to gnash thy ravenous fangs at me! I loathe thee!—
Great and glorious spirit, thou who didst vouchsafe to reveal thyself
unto me, thou who dost know my very heart and soul, why hast thou
linked me with this base associate, who feeds on mischief and revels
in destruction?

MEPH.   Hast done?

FAUST.   Save her! — or woe to thee! The direst of curses on thee for thousands of years!

MEPH.   I cannot loose the bands of the avenger, nor withdraw his bolts. — Save her! — Who was it plunged her into perdition? I or thou?

[FAUST *looks wildly around.*]

Would'st grasp the thunder? Well for you, poor mortals, that 'tis not yours to wield! To smite to atoms the being however innocent, who obstructs his path, such is the tyrant's fashion of relieving himself in difficulties!

FAUST.   Convey me thither! She shall be free!

MEPH.   And the danger to which thou dost expose thyself? Know, the guilt of blood, shed by thy hand, lies yet upon the town. Over the place where fell the murdered one, avenging spirits hover and watch for the returning murderer.

FAUST.   This too from thee? The death and downfall of a world be on thee, monster! Conduct me thither, I say, and set her free!

MEPH.   I will conduct thee. And what I can do, — hear! Have I all power in heaven and upon earth? I'll cloud the senses of the warder, — do thou possess thyself of the keys and lead her forth with human hand! I will keep watch! The magic steeds are waiting, I bear thee off. Thus much is in my power.

FAUST.   Up and away!

SCENE — *Night — Open Country*

FAUST, MEPHISTOPHELES *rushing along on black horses.*

FAUST.   What weave they yonder round the Ravenstone?

MEPH.   I know not what they shape and brew.

FAUST.   They're soaring, swooping, bending, stooping.

MEPH.   A witches' pack.

FAUST.   They charm, they strew.

MEPH.   On! On!

SCENE — *Dungeon*

FAUST. [*With a bunch of keys and a lamp before a small iron door*] A
fear unwonted o'er my spirit falls;
Man's concentrated woe o'erwhelms me here!
She dwells immur'd within these dripping walls;
Her only trespass a delusion dear!
Thou lingerest at the fatal door,
Thou dread'st to see her face once more?
On! While thou dalliest, draws her death-hour near. [*Seizes the
lock.*]

[*Singing within*]

My mother, the harlot,
She took me and slew!
My father, the scoundrel,
Hath eaten me too!
My sweet little sister
Hath all my bones laid,
Where soft breezes whisper
All in the cool shade!

Then became I a wood-bird, and sang on the spray,
Fly away! little bird, fly away! fly away!

FAUST. [*Opening the lock*] Ah! she forebodes not that her lover's near,
The clanking chains, the rustling straw, to hear.   [*He enters.*]
MARG. [*Hiding her face in the bed of straw*] Woe! woe! they come!
oh bitter 'tis to die!
FAUST. [*Softly*] Hush! hush! be still! I come to set thee free!
MARG. [*Throwing herself at his feet*] If thou art human, feel my misery!
FAUST. Thou wilt awake the jailor with thy cry!

[*He grasps the chains to unlock them.*]

MARG. [*On her knees*] Who, headsman, unto thee this power
O'er me could give?
Thou com'st for me at midnight-hour.
Be merciful, and let me live!

Is morrow's dawn not time enough?   [*She stands up.*]
I'm still so young, so young—
And must so early die!
Fair was I too, and that was my undoing.
My love is now afar, he then was nigh;
Torn lies the garland, the fair blossoms strew'd.
Nay, seize me not with hand so rude!
Spare me! What harm have I e'er done to thee?
Oh let me not in vain implore!
I ne'er have seen thee in my life before!

FAUST.   Can I endure this bitter agony?

MARG.   I now am at thy mercy quite.
Let me my babe but suckle once again!
I fondled it the live-long night;
They took it from me but to give me pain,
And now, they say that I my child have slain.
Gladness I ne'er again shall know.
Then they sing songs about me,—'tis wicked of the throng—
An ancient ballad endeth so;
Who bade them thus apply the song?

FAUST.   [*Throwing himself on the ground*] A lover at thy feet bends low,
To loose the bonds of wretchedness and woe.

MARG.   [*Throws herself beside him*] Oh, let us kneel and move the
saints by prayer!
Look! look! yon stairs below,
Under the threshold there,
Hell's flames are all aglow!
Beneath the floor,
With hideous noise,
The devils roar!

FAUST.   [*Aloud*] Gretchen! Gretchen!

MARG.   [*Listening*] That was my lov'd one's voice!

[*She springs up, the chains fall off.*]

Where is he? I heard him calling me.
Free am I! There's none shall hinder me.
To his neck will I fly,
On his bosom will lie!
Gretchen, he called!—On yon threshold he stood;

Amidst all the howling of hell's fiery flood,
The scoff and the scorn of its devilish crew,
The tones of his voice, sweet and loving, I knew.

FAUST. 'Tis I!

MARG.   'Tis thou! O say so once again!   [*Embracing him.*]
'Tis he! 'Tis he! where's now the torturing pain?
Where are the fetters? where the dungeon's gloom?
'Tis thou! To save me thou art come!
And I am sav'd! —
Already now the street I see
Where the first time I caught a glimpse of thee.
There too the pleasant garden shade,
Where I and Martha for thy coming stay'd.

FAUST. [*Endeavouring to lead her away*] Come! come away!

MARG.   Oh do not haste!
I love to linger where thou stayest.   [*Caressing him.*]

FAUST.   Ah haste! For if thou still delayest,
Our lingering we shall both deplore.

MARG.   How, dearest? canst thou kiss no more?
So short a time away from me, and yet,
To kiss thou couldst so soon forget!
Why on thy neck so anxious do I feel —
When formerly a perfect heaven of bliss
From thy dear looks and words would o'er me steal?
As thou wouldst stifle me thou then didst kiss! —
Kiss me!
Or I'll kiss thee!   [*She embraces him.*]
Woe! woe! Thy lips are cold, —
Are dumb!
Thy love where hast thou left?
Who hath me of thy love bereft?

           [*She turns away from him.*]

FAUST.   Come! Follow me, my dearest love, be bold!
I'll cherish thee with ardour thousand-fold;
I but entreat thee now to follow me!

MARG. [*Turning towards him*] And art thou he? and art thou really he?

FAUST. 'Tis I! O come!

MARG.   Thou wilt strike off my chain,
       And thou wilt take me to thine arms again.
       How comes it that thou dost not shrink from me? —
       And dost thou know, love, whom thou wouldst set free?
FAUST.   Come! come! already night begins to wane.
MARG.   I sent my mother to her grave,
       I drown'd my child beneath the wave.
       Was it not given to thee and me — thee too?
       'Tis thou thyself! I scarce believe it yet.
       Give me thy hand! It is no dream! 'Tis true!
       Thine own dear hand! — But how is this? 'Tis wet?
       Quick, wipe it off! Meseems that yet
       There's blood thereon.
       Ah God! what hast thou done?
       Put up thy sword,
       I beg of thee!
FAUST.   Oh, dearest, let the past forgotten be!
       Death is in every word.
MARG.   No, thou must linger here in sorrow!
       The graves I will describe to thee,
       And thou to them must see
       To-morrow:
       The best place give to my mother,
       Close at her side my brother,
       Me at some distance lay —
       But not too far away!
       And the little one place on my right breast.
       Nobody else will near me lie!
       To nestle beside thee so lovingly,
       That was a rapture, gracious and sweet!
       A rapture I never again shall prove;
       Methinks I would force myself on thee, love,
       And thou dost spurn me, and back retreat —
       Yet 'tis thyself, thy fond kind looks I see.
FAUST.   If thou dost feel 'tis I, then come with me!
MARG.   What, there? without?
FAUST.   Yes, forth in the free air.
MARG.   Ay, if the grave's without, — If death lurk there!
       Hence to the everlasting resting-place,
       And not one step beyond! — Thou'rt leaving me?
       Oh Henry! would that I could go with thee!

FAUST. Thou canst! But will it! Open stands the door.

MARG. I dare not go! I've naught to hope for more.
What boots it to escape? They lurk for me!
'Tis wretched to beg, as I must do,
And with an evil conscience thereto!
'Tis wretched, in foreign lands to stray;
And me they will catch, do what I may!

FAUST. With thee will I abide.

MARG.   Quick! Quick!
Save thy poor child!
Keep to the path
The brook along,
Over the bridge
To the wood beyond,
To the left, where the plank is,
In the pond.
Seize it at once!
It fain would rise,
It struggles still!
Save it. Oh save!

FAUST. Dear Gretchen, more collected be!
One little step, and thou art free!

MARG. Were we but only past the hill!
There sits my mother upon a stone —
My brain, alas, is cold with dread! —
There sits my mother upon a stone,
And to and fro she shakes her head;
She winks not, she nods not, her head it droops sore;
She slept so long, she waked no more;
She slept, that we might taste of bliss:
Ah! those were happy times, I wis![1]

FAUST. Since here avails nor argument nor prayer,
Thee hence by force I needs must bear.

MARG. Loose me! I will not suffer violence!
With murderous hand hold not so fast!
I have done all to please thee in the past!

FAUST. Day dawns! My love! My love!

MARG.   Yes! day draws near.
The day of judgment too will soon appear!

---

1. *wis*] know.

It should have been my bridal! No one tell,
That thy poor Gretchen thou hast known too well.
Woe to my garland!
Its bloom is o'er!
Though not at the dance —
We shall meet once more.
The crowd doth gather, in silence it rolls;
The squares, the streets,
Scarce hold the throng.
The staff is broken, — the death-bell tolls, —
They bind and seize me! I'm hurried along,
To the seat of blood already I'm bound!
Quivers each neck as the naked steel
Quivers on mine the blow to deal —
The silence of the grave now broods around!

FAUST.   Would I had ne'er been born!

MEPH.   [*Appears without*] Up! or you're lost.
Vain hesitation! Babbling, quaking!
My steeds are shivering,
Morn is breaking.

MARG.   What from the floor ascendeth like a ghost?
'Tis he! 'Tis he! Him from my presence chase!
What would he in this holy place?
It is for me he cometh!

FAUST.   Thou shalt live!

MARG.   Judgment of God! To thee my soul I give!

MEPH.   [*To* FAUST] Come, come! With her I'll else abandon thee!

MARG.   Father, I'm thine! Do thou deliver me!
Ye angels! Ye angelic hosts! descend,
Encamp around to guard me and defend! —
Henry! I shudder now to look on thee!

MEPH.   She now is judged!

VOICES.   [*From above*]   Is saved!

MEPH.   [*To* FAUST]   Come thou with me!

[*Vanishes with* FAUST.]

VOICE.   [*From within, dying away*] Henry! Henry!